Speed

Advance praise from the climbing community for
Speed Climbing! How to Climb Faster and Better

"Just great! Guess all of our hard-won secrets are out. Guess all my records are going to be taken away now. Great, just freakin' great!"

—Steve Schneider

"Inspiring and joyful! Makes you want to travel light, go fast, and be a better player on the team."

—Tom Frost

"This book is not just for a few, highly skilled climbers who have elevated the sport to a high art. This is for those of us who want to get down without bivying, beat a thunderstorm, or get in a raft of pitches in the few pathetic hours we have available. It is a trove of practical information—detailed yet accessible, sprightly and humorous. Hans Florine is a very great force in our sport. Creative and responsible, he has contributed in more ways than most climbers could know, from setting rad Yosemite and High Sierra records to volunteering for years as the director of the American Sport Climbing Federation. Hans has always been a superior competitor because as hard as he tries to do his best, and to best the next climber, he truly wishes others well. He is the first to congratulate and appreciate a peer who breaks one of his records (then to grab a rope and try again). This book is a way of wishing all of us well."

—Alison Osius, Executive Editor,
Rock and Ice magazine, author, and
former national champion in sport climbing

A**FALCON**GUIDE®

How to Climb™ Series

Speed Climbing!
How to Climb Faster and Better

Second Edition

Hans Florine and Bill Wright

Bruce;
Be quick, see you at the cliff.
Hans Florine

FALCON®

GUILFORD, CONNECTICUT
HELENA, MONTANA
AN IMPRINT OF THE GLOBE PEQUOT PRESS

Text design: Lisa Reneson
Illustrations: Greg Opland
Climbing topo on pages 134–135 courtesy and permission of SuperTopo.

ISSN: 1550-9656
ISBN: 0-7627-3095-1

Manufactured in the United States of America
Second edition/First printing

Contents

Preface

Hans Florine

Here's a challenge: We have received a few reports about how fast our first edition was read cover-to-cover on-sight. The record for the first edition was just more than three hours. Ready? Go!

It's been four years since I wrote the first edition of this book. Since then I have given numerous shows and clinics in which I've praised the stories in our first edition as great ways to motivate or inspire *you* to get out and *get more climbing done*! I have also pointed out the "average Joe" descriptions of my friends in the stories and how they have done extraordinary climbing feats while presumably leading regular lives.

Since the first edition I too have become an " average Joe": I have stayed married; fathered two children; worked a bit more (still not nine to five, but some hourly work); and turned forty years old. What's terrific is that I feel like I'm getting out and doing some of the best climbing and "fitness feats" I've done in my entire life. For example, I've set the speed record on the Nose of El Capitan twice; I've set the speed record on the California fourteeners; I've climbed the Nose and the Regular Route on Half Dome in a day with Peter Coward; I've broken my lifetime best in a mile run—four times; I've run my first marathon; I've ridden my first 100-kilometer bike ride; and I climbed El Capitan for my one-hundredth time!

So what!? Well, it is a revelation to me that while I am supposedly loaded down with more life situations, I'm accomplishing some great climbing goals. This is exactly what this book is about and it should not have been a revelation to me—but it was. Better focus, planning, and execution has made the difference. Now my climbing time is limited, so I anticipate it, plan it, visualize it, and execute it much better.

Getting more in for us is not just about climbing, it's about everything, be it time with the kids, dinner with the wife, or surfing. Greg Crouch wrote me rather boastfully that he left his Conservacion Patagonica office desk at 11:52 a.m. in proper dress for the job. He changed into a wet suit, ran across the parking lot to the beach, paddled out past the break, caught a wave, paddled back out, sat on his board waiting for the next wave, looked down at his watch, and saw that it was noon. Now that's a fine start to a lunch break.

We've removed old and added new stories to this second edition, and kept the ones that we thought were too good to get rid of. We've also made corrections where we saw problems.

Thanks are owed to: Jacqueline Florine, Steve Schneider, Yuji Hirayama, Bill Wright, Steve Gerberding, Russ McBride, Scott Bovard, Peter Coward, Jim Herson, Chandlee Harrell, Greg Murphy, Ammon McNeely, Chris McNamara, Cedar Wright, Brian McCray, Timmy O'Neill, Dean Potter, the Huber brothers, Leo Houlding, Russ Mitrovich, and *many others* who have climbed with me, taught me things, broken my records and inspired me to do better things. You all are part of a community that embraces, in one way or another, the desire to improve on what is possible. For some it's a competitive drive, for others it's the satisfaction from doing what "they said couldn't be done," and for others— they simply love doing tons of climbing and they have limited time.

As before, I truly wish that you will gain knowledge and inspiration from this book so that *you* can get in *more climbing*.

Bill Wright

The struggle itself toward the heights is enough to fill man's heart. One must imagine Sisyphus happy.
—Albert Camus, *The Myth of Sisyphus*

I love climbing—climbing up anything at all. From hiking up a trail to pedaling up steep pavement, from skinning up a snow slope to jamming up a crack, I love to climb. There is something in the struggle against gravity that elates me. I used to think that climbing was a passing fancy and that once I'd climbed El Cap, I'd move on to other adventures. I know now that isn't true. I'm a lifer.

I decided to write this book for many reasons, but the most overwhelming reason was because *I* wanted to have such a book. Despite the fact that speed climbing has a rich history and has been part of our sport since its inception, up until now no book has been available on the subject. I finally figured out that if I wanted such a book, I'd have to write it myself—along with Hans, of course.

This brings me to another reason I wanted to take on this project—the opportunity to work with Hans Florine, the "master of speed climbing." Getting to know Hans and sharing a rope with him has been a thrill, like playing baseball with Babe Ruth.

I have been frequently frustrated by the media's superficial coverage of awesome climbing feats. There seems to be an incredible disregard for the obvious question "How did they go that fast?" Certainly other climbers have wondered the same thing. This book is my attempt to answer that question.

You might be asking yourself, "Who is Bill Wright and why should I read what he's written?" Well, I'm nobody really—but in a sense I'm everybody. At the very least I'm probably a typical weekend climber. But, you ask, "If you're so typical, what do you have to say that might be of interest to me?" I act here mainly as an interviewer, researcher, and writer. I was as curious about the techniques of the super speed climbers as perhaps you are now. While I do practice speed climbing, I do it at a modest level—just like I climb at a modest level. Hence, I'm proof that the techniques in this book aren't just for the superstars, but will prove useful for every weekender in search of more climbing.

While many climbers have influenced me, there is one climber who prompted me to fundamentally reexamine my own climbing—Jim Herson. For years I had been interested in speed climbing, but mostly in an arm-chair manner. However, in June 1999 my partner, Tom Karpeichik, and I were just starting up the Salathé Wall on El Capitan in Yosemite National Park. We were climbing the first ten pitches, known as Free Blast, so that we could fix ropes down from Heart Ledges. We then planned on spending the next three and a half days climbing and hauling our way to the top. This is the standard approach to climbing the Salathé. Our speed was probably about average.

As is often the case, it was a zoo at the start of the route that morning. No less than four parties were jockeying for position on the route. We were there first and moving steadily up the route, but there was another team right on our heels. As I finished leading the fourth pitch, a 5.10b crack, Tom told me that we were going to let another party pass us. I looked down expecting to see the white helmets of the team that had been behind us all morning—but no, the passers were a different party altogether. I was amazed. How could these guys have already passed the White Helmets and now be poised to pass us? They hadn't even hiked to the base of the route by the time I jugged the third pitch, and now they were going by us. I watched as a lean Frank Shorter look-alike practically ran up the 5.10 pitch, only placing a couple pieces of protection. (American Frank Shorter won a gold medal in the Olympic marathon in 1972.) The climber said hello as he clipped a draw into the anchor and, without pausing, moved on up the next pitch! This was my introduction to Jim Herson.

I noticed Herson's climbing rack was tiny—about one-third the size of our rack. He was climbing the Salathé (notorious for wide pitches) with nothing bigger than his single #3 Camalot. We learned from his partner, Peter Coward, that Jim was trying to redpoint the entire Salathé Wall. (At the time only four people had redpointed every pitch on the Salathé: Alex and Thomas Huber, Yuji Hirayama, and Tommy Caldwell. In 2003, Jim finally completed his redpoint.) Clearly Jim was a world-class climber, but that wasn't the most striking aspect of his ascent. What amazed me was that these two were climbing the Salathé in a day. They were climbing it like it was a local crag route, a free-climbing project, like I had done with single-pitch routes near my home. They climbed with a tiny rack and a small pack, and moved lightning fast. It was a different sport than what Tom and I were practicing; we were inching up the rock in painstaking fashion. To compare our ascent to Herson and Coward's is to compare a marathoner with a miler. They were free climbing and moving fast; we were mired in such mundane tasks as jugging fixed lines and hauling bags. It was a big adventure for us, one that we had planned for an entire year; but to Jim it was just the route he'd decided to climb when he woke up that day. I wanted to enter this world and I began researching in earnest. This led to a correspondence and eventually a friendship with Hans, and even Jim Herson.

Speed climbing feats have been reported in a number of books and magazines but never meticulously recorded. I haven't changed that here, but have made an attempt to compile some of its rich history. I've tried to focus on the climbs that have changed attitudes. I have left much out due to limitations of space. Additional sources for speed climbing history can be found in the *2000 American Alpine Club Journal* and *Climbing* magazine issues #153 and #203. I've also left out any history of formal speed competition climbing at this time. I do have visions of writing a more complete history someday, so if you have any information about speed climbing in other areas, please e-mail me at bill@wwwright.com.

I want to acknowledge and thank the great partners I've had throughout the years. In that respect I feel I am probably the luckiest climber in the world. My circle of climbing partners is the best anywhere. I'll risk offending some partners and list names. I'll also apologize ahead of time for anyone left out. Special mention has to go to three partners: Lou "The Loobster" Lorber, George "Trashman" Bell, and Tom "Hardly Manson" Karpeichik. They have an insatiable desire for climbing in all its forms. There are no finer climbers or individuals anywhere. They are the rawest definition of a climbing *partner*. These three will, and have, given me the shirt off their backs. There is no "mine" with them. Everything is *ours*. They never complain, never tire, and never turn down an adventure.

There are many more partners—too many to completely list. I thank Bruce "Dr. Offwidth" Bailey, Eric "Tinky Winky" Winkelman, John "Homie" Prater, Mark "White Rim" Oveson, John "Berries" Black, Greg "Opie" Opland, Steve "Bowling Ball" Mathias, and the rest of the Satan's Minions Scrambling Club for climbing with me.

Of course, I must thank Hans Florine for agreeing to work with me on this book and for his boundless generosity in sharing his home, his knowledge, and his spirit.

Finally, my greatest joy: my family. My wife, Sheri, a serious athlete herself, is the love of my life. She makes it possible for me to pursue climbing. She understands that life is a balancing act and she keeps me from toppling over. She has also given me two great little boys: Daniel and Derek. I can't wait for these two to guide me up Everest—in record time, no less!

When the first edition of this book was published, I was doing speed climbs frequently, but using just the techniques of simul-climbing and simul-seconding, and mostly on smaller crags routes (seven pitches or shorter) around Boulder. Writing the book opened my eyes to what was possible for me and I set my sights on climbing the Nose In A Day (NIAD). Of course, teaming up with Hans would be cheating. He can take literally anyone up the Nose in a day. I needed an equal partner and I convinced Hardly Manson (aka Tom Karpeichik) to join the quest.

We first went to Zion to get a system worked out on smaller walls. We climbed Moonlight Buttress in one day and broke the climb into two blocks: I led the first half and Hardly the second. The first time I ever short-fixed a pitch was on this route. I didn't get very far before Hardly arrived at the belay, and I said to him, "Hey, I've written about such techniques, but I've never actually used them before." I used my own book as a tutorial!

Later that year we did Half Dome in a day, car to car. The next year we returned to Yosemite, broke the Nose into six blocks, and climbed it in just under twenty-two hours. This was an on-sight ascent for Hardly. My first night-leading experience was on the final block, from 8:00 P.M. to 2:00 A.M. I discovered that there is no exposure at night, as my headlamp could only illuminate within a range of 20 feet. After resting on top and waiting for some daylight, we descended the East Ledges, still in our climbing shoes. I even linked the Nose directly into Nutcracker when Opie and the Toolman talked me into joining them.

Later that week we climbed the East Buttress of El Capitan and then I capped the week by climbing the Salathé Wall with Jim Herson in just fifteen hours. Of course, Jim did all the leading and climbed the route mostly free, but I had climbed El Capitan, in a day, three times in one week. This book really works!

CHAPTER 1

SPEED CLIMBING: THE WHAT AND THE WHY

Dream barriers look very high until someone climbs them. Then they are not barriers anymore.
—Lasse Viren, one of the greatest distance runners of all time

What is speed climbing? To some it's what they see on TV—the X Games, where people climb a 60-foot plastic wall in twelve seconds. To others it's plugging away up a 3,000-foot El Cap route in a day. Speed climbing is many different things to many different people, but at its most basic level, speed climbing is a philosophy about moving quickly and efficiently up difficult terrain. It doesn't have to be an all-out race for the world record. Maybe you just want to do a big route in a day. Or, it could just be about setting a personal record on a route—much as you might do while running your favorite trail. This book is not about how to burn the rubber off the bottom of your climbing shoes—it's about getting in more climbing on your climbing days. We wrote this book because we believe that the only thing better than climbing is *more* climbing!

All the tips in this book aren't for everyone to practice. Carefully consider those that you can utilize and discard the others. Keep in mind that the more tips you use, the more climbing you'll do on your weekends—and the bigger your smile will be while you daydream at the office on Monday morning. The desire to improve and learn the more efficient/faster way to do a task can really change what you are able to do in a day—or in an evening after work.

Speed climbing is fun. Speed climbing lets you climb more, but it clearly isn't everything. It holds no interest for some climbers, though most climbers would benefit from at least knowing the techniques and applying them, however sparingly, to their own climbing. We don't speed climb all the time. In fact, for me (B.W.) at least, it is the exception rather than the rule. Legendary French climber, Gaston Rébuffat,

The Snowball Effect of Big Wall Planning

Most people haul tons of gear up an El Cap route not because they want to savor the experience of carrying all that stuff, but because they can't climb the route in one day. Let's take a look at what happens when you can't climb the route in a single day. You have to take bivy gear, right? Maybe a portaledge. Certainly more food and water. Without this extra weight maybe you could do the route in, say, a day and a half; but now it will take you two and a half days because you're going slower hauling all this additional gear and setting up and tearing down the bivouac. So now you need gear for two and a half days, which involves more water and food, slowing you down further. It's the proverbial "snowball effect" of big wall climbing.

wrote in the introduction to his classic book *Starlight and Storm,* ". . . some mountaineers are proud of having done all their climbs without bivouac. How much they have missed!" And despite the fact that Hans sports a license plate that reads "no bivys," we've both taken time to smell the alpine roses.

Speed climbing doesn't mean that you race up the rock so fast that you can't enjoy the climbing or admire the views or revel in the solitude of your position. You could liken it to going on a trail run versus a backpacking trip. On the trail run you are moving much less encumbered and flowing easily over the terrain. You cover the same distance in a long run as on a two-day backpacking trip. Is one better than the other? Not really. It certainly depends on the person. Each experience has its rewards.

Even an average team planning to climb the Nose in three days can benefit from speed climbing techniques. The Nose has good bivy ledges distributed along the route. If you are fast enough to reach these ledges each day, then you won't have to haul up a portaledge or an uncomfortable hammock. This ability to climb fast and get to the bivy ledges means you haul less weight and waste less time setting up and tearing down the bivy. Hence, even though the ascent is not done in a single push, the techniques discussed in this book can increase your enjoyment of the climbing by decreasing the drudgery of hauling unnecessary weight.

Chandlee Harrell in front of Mount Goode on just another weekend outing—if you speed climb. (Gregory Murphy)

Success versus Failure on the Direct North Buttress
by Bill Wright

While getting ready to attempt the Direct North Buttress (DNB) of Middle Cathedral Rock in Yosemite in mid-November, my partner Jim Merritt and I got to talking about the "multiplication of supplies." It started by simply reading the label on our energy bars, which said to "eat one every hour with a quart of water while exercising." "Well," we thought, "we're definitely exercising." We needed to calculate how many bars to bring.

The DNB is a serious, devious route that's 20 pitches long. Jim and I were in over our heads a bit—being somewhat slow climbers—so we decided on a two-day ascent, which meant hauling bivy gear up the route. We would be working about ten hours a day for two days. If we each ate one energy bar per hour with the recommended one quart of water, we calculated the amount of water we would have to haul would equal forty quarts (two people x ten hours x two days x one quart of water). Because there are two pints in a quart and "a pint's a pound the world around," we would have to carry 80 pounds of water alone.

Of course, this is way too much water for a north-facing wall in mid-November, but that's not my point. My point is that if we had hauled 80 pounds of water, it probably would have taken us twice as long to climb the wall—but then we'd have needed to haul twice as many energy bars and twice as much water! You can see where this is leading. Pretty soon we'd be so weighed down that we wouldn't be able to get off the ground.

We could have used siege tactics to climb the DNB and solved our lack-of-speed problem. The first big walls were climbed using siege tactics for exactly this reason. But we didn't want to climb the route that way, not necessarily because of some ethical dilemma—heck, we were just a couple of weekend warriors who weren't trying to prove anything to anybody—but because we didn't have the time or resources for such a prolonged battle.

In the end, we retreated off the DNB. We just weren't fast enough to make the climb and leave ourselves a reasonable safety margin. We didn't really need to be better technical climbers, though of course that would have helped. We just needed to be faster, more efficient climbers.

Reasons to Speed Climb

The reasons for climbing fast are as numerous as the reasons for climbing at all. In alpine climbing, speed is safety. The less time you spend exposed to objective dangers such as avalanches, storms, and rockfall, the safer you are. Maybe you just want to move more efficiently with the least amount of down time. When you call up your partner to make a plan for the weekend, you don't ask, "Want to go belaying tomorrow?" or, "Want to haul a big bag up El Cap this weekend?" No, you want to go climbing! The rest of that crap is just an evil necessity, not a joy to be prolonged.

Climbing fast not only cuts down on the extraneous chores, but it provides for more comfortable nights. When asked why he climbs so fast, the great French speed climber, Jean-Marc Boivin, said, "The fact is that at night I'd rather sleep with Françoise than in a cold bivouac in an ice hole!" Touché.

What about sport climbers doing one- or two-pitch routes without the prospect of a cold bivy? Well, simply put, going faster will make you a better climber. Climbing hard routes at the limit of your ability is frequently a race against muscular failure; the faster you are, the better chance you have to win that race. Getting to the top before you pump out equals success on a sport route.

By far the best reason to speed climb is because it's fun. Remember, the only thing better than climbing is *more* climbing. Climbing fast enables you to climb more pitches, complete more routes, and go more places. Whether that means moving quickly up a route without extraneous distractions or blasting up a route at your absolute limit, speed climbing is fun. As Miles Smart, holder of numerous Yosemite speed records, says, "Stripped down and going light is when [climbing] really becomes fun."

"In Defense of Speed Records . . ."

Some will say that climbing a route to set a speed record is silly and that time is better spent pushing the level of difficulty or forging a new route.

Throwing Tradition to the Wind on the Nose
by Hans Florine

In 1987 I tried to climb the Nose with my buddy Mike Lopez. We got off route on the second pitch and nearly fell to our deaths when a pin came out and left the two of us and the haul bag dangling on *one* small nut. It took us most of the day to get to Sickle Ledge, just four pitches off the ground. We ate some food there and decided that we should bail, so we rappelled the four rope-lengths back to the ground. We made it to the valley floor before dark—barely.

The next year we came back, "weekend warrior bumblies" that we were. We arrived in the meadow Saturday at 6:00 P.M. on the three-day Fourth of July weekend. We were a bit ignorant about "how it's supposed to be done." Despite the fact that it was late in the day, we thought, "What the heck, let's jump on it!" That was at 7:00 P.M. We climbed under a full moon until we couldn't climb any longer. We stopped on Sickle Ledge for a two-hour nap but made it to Dolt Tower by Sunday at noon.

We slept on El Cap Tower in the afternoon for a few hours, continued to climb through the next night, and finally were so whipped we stopped on the ledge at Camp V for six hours of sleep. We topped out on Monday at 1:00 P.M. It was a forty-two-hour ascent—on-sight (kind of). We drank caffeine, drove back home, and made it to classes on Tuesday!

We did this route fast out of necessity, I suppose, but we also did it by saying, "To hell with how it's supposed to be done! We've got two days—let's get on it!" The next time I did the Nose—two years later with Steve Schneider—we made the climb in eight hours. Three years after that I made it to Sickle Ledge with Peter Croft in twenty-six minutes—a distance that took me nearly a day on my first try seven years prior! In 2002, with Yuji Hirayama, it took sixteen minutes.

For some climbers this is undoubtedly true. But just like there are Olympic figure skaters who push the difficulty of their acrobatics each year, there are also Olympic speed skaters who are driven to continually set new world speed records. For some of us, climbing a route quickly, especially on-sight, can be just as adventurous as putting up a new route or climbing a route at the limit of our ability. In fact, it can often be much more of an adventure. A new aid route entails a lot more belaying, hauling, and sleeping on portaledges than it does actual climbing. Speed climbing, on the other hand, maximizes the actual time spent climbing.

Some people are put off by the overtly competitive atmosphere of Yosemite Valley speed climbers. While it's true this atmosphere isn't for everyone, it's also true that many are motivated by competition. In every sport, competition brings out the best in participants. In fact, almost every significant climber's résumé will include at least some mention of a fast time on a particular route. Even sport climbers will mention how fast they redpointed a certain route. Climbing a route fast doesn't require joining some unsanctioned speed competition, it just requires that you enjoy moving quickly over the rock.

Basically, we're firm believers in the power of positive competition. Blatant competition is healthy! It inspires us to do bigger, better, faster feats, and in turn, to inspire others. It creates a feedback loop that drives us to be our best.

Setting speed climbing records is not for everyone. Many people relish the time spent on a wall, and instead of wanting to go faster, seem to stretch things out to prolong their time in the vertical world. El Cap has been climbed in as little as one hour and fifty-one minutes, and as long as thirty-nine days! Some people like to slow down and smell the copperheads; others, as Maverick says in the movie *Top Gun*, just "feel the need—the need for speed!"

Consider a fellow named Jason Wening. Wening isn't a climber; he's a disabled swimmer. But he understands the need for speed—he holds six world records in competitive swimming. When asked why he pushes himself so hard, he responded, "For the simple pleasure of forcing the body and mind I was given to the absolute edge of my capabilities. I'm fascinated by trying to go even faster. And when I do, I get for just a moment a vision of the limitless potential of the human race."

Be Careful Out There (A Disclaimer)

Rock climbing is a dangerous sport, and speed climbing carries with it certain risks. If you don't understand this, then you probably shouldn't be reading this book. Yes, the dangers can be mitigated and we've both climbed thousands of routes without getting killed. (Bill did break his

Best view in the Valley—looking down the Nose from the last pitch. (Hans Florine)

back in a rappelling accident, although he recovered quickly and three months later broke the record for climbing the "Top Ten" Flatiron routes with Tom Karpeichik.) Speed climbing does not necessarily result in unsafe climbing. The point is that you can get away with taking risks time after time, but don't get lulled into a false sense of security.

As Bill's experience emphasizes, accidents do happen, so don't let your guard down. In a sport such as tennis, if you make a mistake, the worst that can happen is you lose the point. In climbing, a bad mistake can kill you. In tennis you have a split second to make a decision and execute a shot, and it is difficult to be "on" every time under these rapid-fire circumstances. In climbing, you have plenty of time to make the right decision. There is no time limit in most cases. Even though this book is about climbing faster, these speed techniques must be tempered with good common sense. Take enough time to make sure you and your partner are safe. Be certain that you are doing everything right, and then recheck everything again. If things look good, continue from there.

During a speed ascent of the Nose with Dean Potter, Timmy O'Neill once made a near fatal mistake. Timmy was cleaning a pendulum pitch and had lowered out with a loop of rope. He hadn't tied in short because he had his jugs on the rope instead. Just before he let go of his lower-out loop, he felt something was wrong, but he was feeling the pressure to move fast. He let go of the loop and took a hundred-foot fall onto the end of the rope. He was unhurt, but should have taken the time to notice that his jugs were on the wrong section of the rope.

You'll find as you read through the book that we don't advocate rushing decisions; we have you eliminate unnecessary actions and methods and make more efficient movements. In some cases, climbing fast is safer than climbing slowly. For instance, if a bad storm is approaching, it is advantageous to move fast so that you can get off the climb, either up or down, and seek shelter.

Having said that, we want you to remember that some of the techniques specified in this book can be dangerous if you don't use good judgment when implementing them. Decide which techniques will work for you, take what you can from this book, and use it to get in tons of climbing—but be careful!

Crazy Eights

by Bill Wright
Sunday, June 3, 2001

This was my only day to climb with Hans and, not surprisingly, he wanted to push the speed a bit. His idea was to climb as many Tuolumne Meadows domes as we could before dinner. It was a hobbit's approach: We wanted adventure, but above all we didn't want to be late for dinner, which in our case would be at the Tioga Pass Restaurant (TPR). We got up at 5:15 A.M. and so did Hardly and Judy—they were planning to climb up at Tuolumne also. Hans and I ate and took off in his car. After climbing he'd be continuing on to the eastern side of the Sierra to meet up with his family and some friends. We'd meet Hardly and Judy for dinner and I'd go back with them.

We pulled up below Stately Pleasure Dome just after 7:00 A.M., but spent so long changing clothes, gearing up, and, most of all, looking for Hans's chalk bag, that Hardly and Judy pulled up before we even left the car. Judy immediately asked, "So, how many domes have you climbed so far?" She's a pistol . . .

I put on my climbing shoes at the car since the approach and descent involves friction climbing on steep slabs. Hans went with a pair of running shoes, which he had resoled with sticky rubber. He'd use these for the first four domes of the day. We finally started up just before 7:30 A.M.

I'd do most of the leading throughout the day, since that is the safest arrangement for us to simul-climb—Hans isn't likely to fall on anything I can climb.

Many years ago I had climbed South Crack and found it very easy for the 5.8 rating. Today was no different. It seemed ludicrous to compare this route to some of the 5.8 off-width and chimney routes in the valley. I'm not a great slab climber, but this slab was low angle *and* it had a crack in it. I guessed the crux friction moves were 5.8, but the route wasn't sustained. It was just plain fun.

We romped up the route at a good pace, and for our descent we used a neat trick. I went above the big pine tree at the start of the descent slabs and weighted the rope. I got a cushy lowering down the slab, while Hans got a pull up the slab to the tree. We were back at the car as Hardly started up the first pitch. Judy waved good-bye to us as we hopped in the car and sped off.

Our next dome, Pywiack, was just up the road. The easiest route on this dome is the Dike Route (5.9)—a fun, run-out friction route that follows a knobby dike. We parked and as soon as we hit the low-angle slabs at the base, we started our route time. I started to tie into the rope and Hans said, "Tie in while you're hiking up this slab. Always keep moving." He's a nut, but I obliged.

I'd done this route once before also and had trouble finding the bolts on it. This time the same thing happened. I missed a bolt and was run out 40 feet or so. I couldn't see another bolt until the belay, another 50 feet. I wrestled with this dilemma a bit and decided to go on. Thankfully, as soon as I made this decision I noticed a bolt near me. This turned out to be very good since the moves above were challenging.

We simul-climbed, with me leading once again, through the crux 5.9 section, then I clipped into the anchors and belayed Hans up the crux. He was still climbing in his running shoes, and every time I'd look back down the route to him, he'd be climbing with no hands, adjusting the slack with his Grigri. Clearly he wasn't too challenged. We didn't do the final 5.7 crack pitch. Most parties don't do it—maybe because it requires gear and is of a very different nature. I think the descent is a lot longer also. We didn't go to the top of most domes anyway. We just descended the slabs to the west back to the base.

To get as many domes as possible, we tried to add in short routes whenever we could. Our first opportunity was with the Golfer's Route on Low Profile Dome. This route has a short approach, is only two pitches long, and is rated only 5.7. I combined the route into one pitch, which isn't a big stretch since together they are only 165 feet long. Nevertheless, Hans simul-climbed behind me. His philosophy about simul-climbing isn't what you'd normally think. For most climbers, simul-climbing is something that is done when you run out of rope and want to keep moving. Hans starts moving long before the rope runs out. His philosophy is for both climbers to keep moving as much as possible. Why just sit at the base when you can be moving? Most respond that one climber needs to be attached to a bomber anchor at all times. Hans's response: Standing on solid ground is a bomber anchor. If you aren't confident that you can hold your ground when the leader falls, you should not simul-climb. Also, bomber gear placed between the climbers should be sufficient to keep both climbers from hitting the ground—but not much else. Is this more dangerous than regular climbing? Yes, but it is faster as well.

It is important to note that there is not extra slack for the leader in this situation. The Grigri turns the rope into an infinitely adjustable length of rope (up to the maximum, of course). Hence, Hans always climbs with a loop of rope beneath him. It takes careful management to ensure this doesn't get caught on a flake and impede progress.

I clipped the chains at the top and Hans immediately lowered me to the first belay. Hans went up and tagged the anchor and I lowered him down. Hans only brought his Grigri, which cannot be used to rappel on a doubled rope. So, I did my first simul-rappel. Hans slapped the Grigri on one end of the rope and I put my belay device on the other. We clipped a sling between us to ensure we stayed together, and down we went. This worked great and was fun.

Next up were the two most crowded routes, and we expected other parties. We'd have our diplomatic skills put to the test in negotiating passage. First was West Crack on DAFF (Dome Across From Fairview) Dome. This is a fun route with one 5.9 move down low and the rest of the route 5.8 or easier. The second pitch is particularly memorable as it passes an overhanging bulge via tricky hand-crack moves and some big jugs.

Sure enough, when we arrived at the base there were two climbers at the top of the first pitch and a third was halfway up the first pitch. We could have climbed Crescent Crack (10a), but I found that route continuously hard. West Crack is much easier, so we decided to climb up to the party and ask if we could simul-climb through. I prefer to let Hans handle situations like this, since many climbers recognize him and get a kick out of letting him fly by. A bumbler like myself doesn't get the same reaction, but once again I was on the sharp end.

I tried to look competent and fast as I approached the belay. It was cold and windy and I noticed the leader of the party was in shorts. I knew they wouldn't want to be held up under such conditions. I certainly wouldn't. When I was about 20 feet below them, and before I had a chance to initiate a conversation, the leader called down to me, "It's pretty crowded up here." His tone indicated a bit of annoyance and I immediately felt guilty. I sheepishly said, "Yeah, that's true. I'll bet it's cold up there also." I hesitated a second, then meekly said, "We were wondering if we could simul-climb through." The leader was a bit surprised by this and asked, "Are you simul-climbing now?"

Now, I wasn't at the first belay so Hans probably hadn't left the ground yet, but I knew the only way to answer this question was affirmatively. The leader responded, "Well, if you're already simul-climbing you might as well come through."

I thanked him immediately and said how nice he was to let us pass. After a brief pause he said, "Yes, I am nice to let you climb through, but I don't appreciate you guys coming up here when you knew what we were doing." I didn't want to be an asshole and I didn't want to push on past if it meant bad feelings among climbers. I was excited about linking up a bunch of domes, but not at the cost of pissing people off. Lots of parties are very friendly and let you pass, if it doesn't inconvenience them much. Others won't allow it at all. I told him, "Look, I don't have to climb through. I just came up here to ask if it would be okay. I can put in an anchor right where I am, below your belay, and we can rap off. You were here first and I just came up to ask. I didn't invade your belay."

He encouraged me to climb through and softened his tone considerably. His partners seemed happy to let me by. As I approached the belay, I leaned my head back to look up at the steep second pitch and my helmet fell off, bouncing all the way to the ground. I had put the helmet on at the car for the hike in, but hadn't snapped the buckle. That had to give these guys a sense of confidence. Yup, a real competent climber coming through! He doesn't even know how to put on his helmet!

Hans yelled up, "Do we need to get that now or on the way down?" At the time he was a bit concerned about doing the opening 5.9 moves in his tennis shoes, and was glad to hear me say, "On the way down." We didn't have any choice about that; we had to climb past this party now.

I climbed through the belay and over the fun, overhanging start of the second pitch. I told the other climbers to say hi to Hans when he came up. I was hoping they'd figure out who Hans was, but it didn't dawn on them. I climbed about two and a half pitches before setting a natural belay anchor and putting Hans on belay. Soon Hans had climbed up to me, grabbed the rack, and was leading above me—tennis shoes smearing on the rock. We simul-climbed the rest of the way to the top, switched shoes, and ran down the steep descent slabs to the base of the route to retrieve my helmet. Looking up, the second climber was just starting to follow the second pitch. We yelled our encouragement and ran back to the car.

Our next dome was the biggest of the day and had previously been an all day climb for me. Fairview Dome was just a little ways up the road. We were surprised to only see two cars at the parking area and hoped the climbers from both wouldn't be on the Regular Route. Before we left the road, we saw a climber at the first belay and upon our arrival at the base, he was still there. His second was about halfway up the first pitch and, sure enough, the other party was gearing up at the base. I'd let Hans handle the negotiations.

Hans walked up to the party at the base and introduced himself, "Hi, I'm Hans. What are your names?" They responded Ray and

Leslie. As Ray started to lead the first pitch, he asked, "Hans, what's your last name?" Hans said, "Christian Anderson," then smiled and said, "Florine." Ray said, "Hey, I know Nancy Feagin (Hans's former girlfriend) real well. I used to climb with her a lot." Hans said, "Then you might know that she just recently summited Everest." They went on for a bit and then Ray went back to leading. Hans told Leslie that we were trying to do a bunch of domes in a day, to which she replied, "Then I suppose you want to just climb over the top of us." Hans said, "What I want and what I get are two different things. You were here first and you have dibs on the route." She said she wouldn't mind. Hans yelled up to ask Ray and he said, "No problem, come on up."

So I geared up and started up behind him. I climbed a variation crack about 5 feet left of the main crack so that our ropes would stay separated a bit. Eventually, I had to merge with the main crack just before the crux move and our ropes ran more on top of each other. I stayed a safe distance below him so I wouldn't be in danger of him falling on me, and so as not to be rude.

As we approached the belay ledge, Ray told the other party that his plan was to climb above them to an alternate belay, but that the guy behind him (me) was climbing a lot faster and he planned to let me pass at this ledge, since we had promised to simul-climb the first couple of pitches. I tried to move by as quickly as possible, thanking them all as I moved straight up the next pitch.

I ran the first four pitches together up to Crescent Ledge. Upon arrival I had three pieces on my rack and no slings—two went in for the belay. I was just starting to get worried about what I'd belay with when I came across the ledge. The climbing was so fun on these opening pitches that I just didn't want to stop. Finally, out of gear, I had to.

Hans, never far behind, soon joined me on the ledge and said, "Well, you've had a chance to rest, so why don't you continue leading?" I led off and we simul-climbed the next eight pitches to the top without regearing. What a fun ramble the route was! Hans joined me on the summit one hour and eleven minutes after I started up the first pitch. Once again, we trotted down the slabs in back and along the base of the wall and back to the car—completing the climb in just more than two hours car-to-car.

It was time for another small dome, and the sport-climbing area of East Cottage Dome was just up the road. The approach to this crag is a bit longer than some of the other domes, but we made it in about twenty minutes. This small dome has increasingly harder sport routes as you move from right to left along the base of the wall. The climbs also get a bit longer as you move left. The easiest and shortest route is called Knobulator, rated 10c, and has only four bolts leading up to the anchor, 60 feet away.

As we arrived, a woman, Miss Lena, was climbing the upper half of Knobulator. We introduced ourselves to Trevor, her belayer, and I changed shoes. We asked if it was okay to start leading the route while Miss Lena set up her rappel. They said it was no problem, and I headed up.

Rushing a bit too much and deftly combining this error with little skill and no forearm endurance, I pitched off the route at the crux for a 15-foot fall. I immediately got back on the route and climbed a bit more thoughtfully to the anchors, just barely making it before my arms gave out again. I lowered and cleaned the route, then Hans cruised up it. We changed back into our approach shoes and ran back to the car.

We drove to our final stop at the Lembert Dome parking lot and took a bit of a siesta. Hans got out his big sun hat and a bedroll and relaxed for some lunch. Leafing through the guidebook, I noticed a three-pitch 5.8 route on something called Dog Dome. That seemed like an easy way to tick off another dome, and we decided to do it before Lembert. We asked a climber in the parking lot if they had ever done it and they said, "We tried once, but couldn't find it. Then a second time we found it, but didn't climb it because it didn't look that good." We could hardly ask for a better recommendation than that. We were both salivating at the prospect of bagging the route.

Hiking in to Dog Dome, I looked back at Hans, and he didn't look too excited about things. I asked how he felt and he said, "Sick." He sat down on the ground and looked tired. I had never seen Hans tired before. I thought, "Wow, I tired out Hans Florine. What a stud I am." Of course that wasn't the case, and roles would soon be reversed.

After a brief rest Hans agreed to continue on for ten minutes. If we didn't find the dome within that time, we'd turn back. We found it within the allotted time, but it took more like twenty minutes to actually get to the base of the route. Indeed, the route did look serious. It started with a 7-inch crack, as expected, but it was rife with lichen and a bit damp. A small snowfield barred dry access to the route. I placed a number of large stones across the field and changed shoes.

I found the first pitch quite serious despite the 5.7 rating. The climbing was definitely hard and the protection was scant. I ran out 150 feet of rope to a ledge with a couple of rusty pitons and decided to belay. The crack above looked difficult. It was irregular and filled with sharp crystals. When Hans arrived I told him to lead through. He agreed that the climbing was somewhat serious.

I followed the 5.8 jam crack and found it pretty sustained. The crux was a short, 10-foot chimney section. The rock wasn't very solid here and the protection was tiny TCUs. I was glad Hans had led. Hans put the second two pitches together so we were now on the summit. The descent was trivial and we were soon headed back for Lembert, but the climb had taken some of the wind out of my sails. My motivation was waning and when we got to Lembert, I looked wistfully up at Cry In Time Again, a 5.9 bolted route.

Unfortunately, it had a party on it. We decided to do the Direct Northwest Face (10c with a thin crack crux) instead.

I told Hans, "I'm fading. I'll lead the first three pitches (fourth class, 5.8, 5.9) and you can lead the last two (10a, 10c), okay?" Hans said that would be fine and I started up at a much slower pace than I had been maintaining. I was also placing more gear. We simul-climbed these pitches and once again Hans was mostly climbing without his hands.

The 5.9 section didn't seem too bad and soon I was standing below the 10a hand-crack pitch. This is a short pitch and I was feeling better, so I called down to Hans that I'd do the next pitch also, as I had plenty of gear left on the rack. The crux is indeed short here, but it is burly and I had to crank hard to lock off my high jam and reach the finishing jug. I pulled onto the ledge and looked at the final 10c pitch. It was a thin crack and also didn't appear to be very long. There was a fixed wired nut near the top, and I decided to continue once again. This would prove to be a mistake.

I placed a good stopper from the ledge and then moved up 4 feet or so and placed what I thought to be an okay stopper. A few more feet and I clipped the fixed wired. It looked manky, but I had two pieces below it. I launched into the crux fingerlocks and tried to race for the top. I was about 5 feet above the fixed piece when I peeled off, expecting a short fall. But I didn't stop short. I kept going, falling out from the wall. Bam! I slammed into the ledge with my back and my arm, and then fell off that before I stopped. I was shocked. What had happened? My arm hurt. I righted myself and Hans yelled up to see if I was okay. I said I was all right and pulled myself onto the ledge. I discovered that I had pulled the wire completely out of the fixed piece and then pulled my upper stopper also. The lower stopper caught my fall.

Hans asked, "How's your back?" I said my back didn't hurt, but my arm did. I considered finishing the pitch, and Hans said, "Bring me up to that ledge while you think about it."

By the time he arrived I had decided that I had had enough for the day and let him lead. He found the pitch challenging also and jammed in a couple of small TCUs, admonishing me as he went to use cams. Above he climbed a somewhat unprotected slab, but I was soon on belay. We didn't have a nut tool with us (yes, that isn't smart when carrying nuts) and I couldn't clean the stopper that had caught my fall. I left it and continued up the pitch. Mimicking Hans's movements, I climbed the pitch clean.

We hiked off to the south down the smooth slabs of the dome. As we approached the parking lot, I noticed two figures watching us from a picnic table. Sure enough, it was Hardly and Judy. They had done two routes on Stately Pleasure Dome (South Crack and the Great White Book) and two routes on Low Profile Dome (Golfer's Route and Darth Vader's Revenge) and then relaxed. We were all ready to head for some dinner.

We spent a total of 4:44 climbing, averaging about 7.5 minutes for both of us to climb each pitch. We spent 1:39 either driving, drinking, eating, etc. at the car. The remaining 4:05 was spent hiking to and from each route. Judging from the time spent hiking, I'd guess we hiked about 12 miles. Without my trusty altimeter watch I can only guess at the total vertical: 6,000 feet. The total time for the outing was ten hours and twenty-eight minutes. That seems like a pretty long day and I was certainly dragging on the last route, but it didn't seem that bad until the end. Breaking the day up into so many smaller sections with nice breaks at the car made it seem easier.

What a great day it was. Moving fast over such exquisite rock with a great, enthusiastic partner is a wonderful experience. Tuolumne is a beautiful place and the weather was perfect. We met some very friendly folk, and they smiled at our crazy antics. I was wiped out at the end of the day, but that's satisfying.

At the TPR we sat next to the two climbers that were on Cry In Time Again. We told them we were the climbers to their right, and they said, "Wow, you guys were moving really fast."

Dome	Left car	Base of route	Top of route	Back at car	Total Route Time	Total pitches
South Crack on Stately Pleasure Dome (5.8, 6 pitches)	7:26 A.M.	7:30 A.M.	7:57 A.M.	8:04 A.M.	27 min.	6
Dike Route on Pywiack (5.9, 4 pitches)	8:09 A.M.	8:12 A.M.	8:39 A.M.	8:48 A.M.	27 min.	10
Golfer's Route on Low Profile Dome (5.7, 2 pitches)	8:57 A.M.	9:01 A.M.	9:15 A.M.	9:20 A.M.	14 min.	12
West Crack on DAFF Dome (5.9, 6 pitches)	9:34 A.M.	9:50 A.M.	10:16 A.M.	10:35 A.M.	26 min.	18
Regular Route on Fairview Dome (5.9, 11 pitches)	10:47 A.M.	11:12 A.M.	12:23 P.M.	12:51 P.M.	1 hour, 11 min.	29
Knobulator on East Cottage Dome (5.10c, 1 pitch)	1:08 P.M.	1:26 P.M.	1:46 P.M.	1:58 P.M.	20 min.	30
North Face of Dog Dome (5.8, 3 pitches)	2:10 P.M.	3:28 P.M.	4:03 P.M.	N/A	35 min.	33
Direct Northwest Face of Lembert Dome (5.10c, 5 pitches)	N/A	4:31 P.M.	5:35 P.M.	5:54 P.M.	1 hour, 4 min.	38

CHAPTER 2
MULTIPITCH CLIMBS

Why should I practice running slow? I already know how to run slow. I want to learn to run fast.

—Emil Zatopek, winner of three gold medals in the 1952 Olympics

This chapter doesn't attempt to describe everything involved in climbing multipitch routes. John Long and Craig Luebben's book *Advanced Rock Climbing* is a good reference for climbing systems, belaying, descending, equipment, etc. We are going to deal with techniques that are specific to speed climbing. You will learn a variety of ways to increase your speed. In Long and Luebben's book, there is a line about simul-climbing (a technique discussed in our Chapter 4) that reads ". . . whatever situation might force you into simul-climbing, vaya con Dios." Go with God! Well, that's not our sentiment. We will share "fringe" techniques that allow you to move fast.

Getting Started

Every type of climbing is potentially dangerous, and speed climbing isn't any different; but if you are afraid, you won't be able to move as fast as you can. You should know your safety system so well that you can make last-minute changes without hesitation. At belays you want to stay clipped into two independent and secure links, but these two links might not be what you're used to.

When climbing fast on multipitch routes, the typical sequence of events should go something like this. The lead climber blasts up the pitch with reckless abandon . . . That's what you expected right? Going fast by being reckless? No, the leader moves efficiently and safely up the pitch and yells down a one-minute (or two-minute) warning as she gets close to the next anchor. This allows the belayer to get ready to move by breaking down unnecessary anchor points, putting on his backpack, lacing up

Chandlee Harrell having fun on a day-long push up Tis-sa-ack. (Gregory Murphy)

his shoes—getting ready to rock. The instant the leader says "Off belay," and then "Rope fixed" or "On belay," the follower can start up.

Up to now, it's been assumed that there is a fixed anchor station at the end of the pitch, or at least a clear belay location. In the event that there is no clear belay, the second might yell "30 feet!" so the leader knows she's approaching the end of the line. This gives the leader time to decide where to set up a belay. Occasionally you will not find a solid belay spot before running out of rope. If this situation is likely to occur, you should discuss a plan of action with your partner before leaving the ground. The likely outcome may be to simul-climb until you reach a suitable belay.

It should be standard procedure for the belayer to call out "Halfway!" when half of the rope has been consumed by the leader. This gives the leader some idea of her climbing rate and her location on the pitch. She can use this information to decide where to belay and how to use the remaining pieces on the rack.

Leader Responsibilities

1. Once at the anchor, the leader should get herself off belay so the second can start getting ready to move. The key to climbing fast is keeping both climbers as busy as possible. When the leader reaches the belay location, the belayer can't do anything productive until the leader calls down "Off belay." Then the belayer can take the belay device off and work on leaving the lower belay location.

2. The leader should fix the rope for the follower or put him on belay. The goal is to accomplish this before the second is ready to climb—eliminating wasted time waiting for a belay. When belaying the second, pull up all slack BEFORE the belay device is attached.

3. The leader should get the haul bag (if there is one) off the lower anchor and prepare to haul so the belayer can completely take down the lower anchor.

4. If the second is climbing rather than jugging, the leader should haul the bag to the top anchor and belay at the same time.

5. The leader should set the haul bag so it is ready for the next lead.

6. The leader should be organizing the ropes and gear, placing the first pieces of the next pitch, or getting the pieces ready.

7. Finally, the leader should eat, drink, and get comfortable.

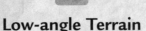

Low-angle Terrain

A lot of time can be lost setting up belays. While belays are crucial, it is not always necessary to have three equalized pieces. In fact, it is sometimes quite sufficient and safe to have *no* pieces in the belay at all. If the leader can drop down over an edge or crouch in between boulders, she can adequately belay a second on low-angle terrain. In this situation a hip belay can be faster and just as satisfactory as a traditional belay.

Frequently I (B.W.) encounter this situation in the Flatirons above Boulder. Many of the climbs are fairly low-angle, and I often lead all the pitches. If I'm comfortable soloing the ground, I can run up a route much faster using this technique. A follower that falls on a low-angle slab with no slack in the rope does not put much force on the rope and can easily be held with a hip belay. Practice this!

The key to moving fast isn't necessarily climbing without protection or without a belay, but being able to switch quickly from simul-soloing to simul-climbing to belayed climbing and back again based on the terrain.

Equipment

Double duty can be tricky. How do you put on the pack and tie your shoes while you are belaying the leader? How do you haul the bag and belay the second at the same time? Practice is one answer, but modern technology helps a lot as well. Using a Grigri to belay allows the belayer to drop his hands from the device without the risk of dropping the climber (or you can use a Trango Cinch as a substitute for the Grigri). It is ironic that the Grigri has found the most use in two widely disparate subcultures of climbing: sport climbing and speed climbing.

Rock Exotica's Wall Hauler or Petzl's Mini Traxion are also extremely handy for hauling the bag. These simple devices are light and easy to use. Combine the Grigri with the Wall Hauler, and hauling and belaying simultaneously becomes a reasonable chore. The Kong Gi-Gi and the Petzl Reverso also allow for toprope belaying where hands-free moments do not sacrifice a safe belay.

Leading in Blocks

Climbing can be tiring, and you don't climb as fast when you're tired. You could think of climbing in the traditional manner as a series of intervals. When "swinging leads," the leader works his way up the pitch and gets to rest while the follower climbs the pitch. The follower is perhaps tired upon reaching the belay but still must plunge directly into the next lead.

Once, I (B.W.) was climbing Pervertical Sanctuary on the Diamond of Longs Peak. My partner, George, had just followed the crux pitch and was too pumped to lead the next pitch, which was also quite hard. I led it so that we could keep moving. At the next belay, the same thing happened, only this time, a storm was imminent. George could have led the next pitch, but I was fresher and would be faster, and now we really needed the speed. The hail storm hit us minutes after I finished the final lead.

Frequently, swinging leads isn't the most optimal way to climb—for speed, or even for redpointing. Also, there is a certain amount of mental preparation that goes into leading. Once a climber is in that mode, it is sometimes more efficient to stay in there.

Leading in blocks is a way to preserve leader mind-set and momentum, and to allow the most rested climber to move first. A block is a consecutive collection of pitches led by the same leader. When the Nose was first climbed in a day, it was broken up into three giant blocks; each block was assigned to the most proficient climber for the type of climbing in that block. This allowed one person to psyche up for the duties of moving the team quickly up the wall, giving his all before dropping into a supportive role. Since then, this technique has been used more often than not on speed ascents.

How long is a block? The route and the team will dictate how the route is broken into blocks. A block might be as few as a couple of pitches on a short route, 10 pitches on a big wall, or even 31 pitches, as on the speed record ascent of the Nose. Leading can be stressful; it can be very satisfying; and it can be both at the same time. How long a person stays in the lead will depend on a lot of factors including the following: Does the leader need a break from the stress? Has the team reached an agreed upon pitch or time allotment for the leader? Is there a good ledge to perform the switch? Has the climbing changed character, now requiring the skills of the other partner?

Belays and Changeovers

When the leader yells, "Two minutes," the follower gets everything ready so she can jump on the ascenders or climb the pitch. If the anchor is bomber, I usually take it all down, but remain clipped to one good piece. When the leader is at the top anchor and the follower is at the bottom anchor, no upward progress is being made. Don't let this last long—do something to change it!

A classic problem happens when the climber at the top anchor yells "Off belay," and the bottom climber doesn't hear the leader. They both sit there for fifteen minutes before one says, "Hey, are you climbing or what?" Be sure every verbal or signal command you give your partner gets answered. For "Off belay," answer "Okay, you're off belay." For any command ("Rope is fixed," "Bag ready to haul," etc.) at least give an "Okay" in response so that your partner knows that you heard her.

It's best to agree with your partner on verbal commands prior to climbing. You should use definitive words, and maybe even decide on a set number of syllables for each command. This way a garbled command will not be mistaken for a different command. Don't use "Yeah" and "Nay," instead use "Yes" and "No." If your lead partner yells "I'm off belay," don't answer "Off belay!" Your partner might think you're asking, "Off belay?" There is less chance of misunderstanding if you answer "Okay, belay *is* off." When you're at a busy cliff, follow all verbal communication with your partner's name. "You're off belay, Bill." Consider walkie-talkies for even better communication.

On a route when verbal communication is impossible, establish a set of "rope commands" with your partner. I have a set of rope commands that I use with all my regular partners. It never hurts to review these commands at the start of a climb. I use three sharp tugs on the rope to mean "off belay." Two more sharp tugs on the rope means the follower is "on belay." When in doubt the second should wait for the rope to come tight to make sure he is on belay. Move up a bit (ideally still clipped to the anchors), and see if the rope becomes tight again. An important note: Only the leader uses these rope commands. The second should never pull sharply on the rope for obvious reasons.

If the follower is jugging and not leading the next pitch, she should stay on the ascenders upon arriving at the belay anchor and resist clipping into the anchor immediately (see Figure 2-1). Remember the goal is to get the leader moving as soon as possible. The follower just trusted her jugs for the whole pitch; why not just hang on them while the leader gets set to go?

The second unclips her end of the rope, gives it to the leader, and immediately puts him on belay. Switching ends of the rope is key because the follower's end of the rope is hanging free from the belay and is ready to go immediately. There is no need to go through the sometimes complex process of unweighting the belay so that the leader can get unclipped. Also, when the second clips into the leader's end, she is already anchored to the belay. I cannot stress enough how easy and fast this makes changeovers—especially at hanging belays.

While the second is doing this, the leader can be pulling gear off the follower and arranging it on her harness or rack. These two jobs can be done by both follower and leader. Do what works best for your circumstances, but keep both of the climbers working when you're at the anchor. It may be that the leader or follower is still hauling while the other is racking and preparing for the leader to leave the belay. If the leader is ready to go, and the bag is not at the anchor, *and* there is little or no chance of the bag getting stuck, then the leader can start off while the belayer simultaneously hauls and belays. Of course, the hauling device must be returned to the leader before she gets too far along.

Remember: When both or all the climbers are at the anchor, everyone should be doing something! This is a point where no upward progress is being made, so don't let it last long. Bust your butts to get the leader off the anchor. This is a perfect example of shaving two to thirty minutes off a pitch. Yes, I've seen changeovers at a hanging belay take thirty minutes or more. Feel a sense of urgency here; it won't last long. Once the leader is off and gaining altitude, there will be plenty of time for the belayer to relax. Develop a set routine for belay anchor and changeover activities.

Once the leader leaves the anchor, the belayer should be moving ascenders off the rope and going direct to the anchor. The belayer's primary responsibility is to keep the leader moving. To this end, her first task should be to organize gear and ropes. Once this is done, she can start eating and drinking.

An alternative to using two carabiners is to have the leader pull up all, or some, of the rope before fixing. When the follower arrives at the anchor, he can send the leader off on that section of rope, then work to unclip the knots from the anchor *while* belaying.

FIGURE 2-1

Second jugs to anchor and then stays on the ascenders to swap gear, switch ends of rope, and belay for leader.

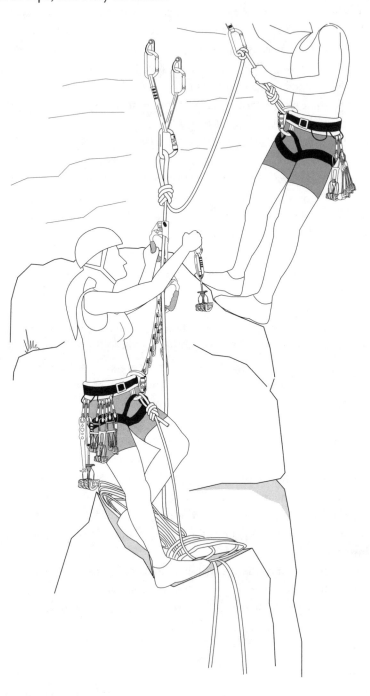

Hans lowering out of the pendulum from Sickle to the Dolt Hole crack. Note that Hans is following this pitch, not leading it. (Tom Evans)

A final note: Be efficient about the gear transfer. Incidentally, most people not only call it the "handoff" of gear, they actually hand off the gear to each other. This is a waste of movement. Why not just clip the gear onto the leader? The leader could pull gear off you and clip it to herself while you're also clipping gear to her, or doing something else.

Three-person Aid Teams

Have the leader take up a trail line. When the leader arrives at the belay anchor, she should fix the ropes. When the second gets to the leader, she can take over the lead or belay the first leader on the line she just jugged. When the third climber arrives, the leader can build a quick temporary

Joe Terravecchia on the No Escape Apron in the Tetons. (George I. Bell)

anchor and lower a loop of slack down to retrieve the other rope end and any gear cleaned from the last pitch.

If a party has three ropes, the leader can haul a bag on the third line while the two followers are jugging. The follower that is likely to get to the leader first should bring up the end of the trail line if they are not hauling on the third line. A pitch that might take forty minutes or more to clean only takes five minutes to jug on a free line.

If the leader put in a ton of gear and has little or no gear left to start leading the next pitch, make sure the person jugging the free line takes any gear possible from the lower anchor and pulls out any gear along the pitch that is easy to clean. Then the leader has some gear and can continue up while you're waiting for the person cleaning the pitch below.

The free-line jugger often can remove pieces above the person cleaning the pitch, which makes the swing on traverses go easier. The opposite is true as well; clean accordingly. When a pitch is overhanging, consider clipping in the trail line a few times during the pitch because it is easier and faster when the follower can "drive" off the wall while jugging.

2:48!
by Hans Florine

Yuji Hirayama stayed at my Yosemite home for a few weeks in the fall of 2002. As usual, he was cruising most of the hardest free climbing routes all over Yosemite. Since I had helped Yuji on a few of his projects over the years, he thought to offer running up the Nose with me for a lark. Yuji had done it earlier that year with his friend Tomatsu in a respectable sub eight-hour time. Timmy O'Neill and Dean Potter held the current record at 3:24, set in the fall of 2001.

I drove up to Yosemite from the San Francisco Bay Area on the eve of September 20, and Yuji and I set off up the Nose early the next morning. We passed no less than seven parties as we simul-climbed, short-fixed, counter-weighted; we used all our tricks and sped to a time of 3:27! We figured that you should get a one-minute "deduction" for each party passed, so we should be "awarded" the record time, no? NOT! We knew we couldn't pull that shenanigan.

Yuji had a huge smile on his face from that ascent and he was stunned that we turned in such a fast time. He was hooked! Yuji had me come up again from the Bay Area on the eve of September 28, and on the morning of September 29, Yuji and I climbed the Nose on El Capitan again.

Yuji led the whole route. We simul-climbed about 2,450 feet, and I jugged while Yuji short-fixed and self-belayed for about 500 feet. Except for our friends, Bill and Lou, at the top of the first pitch taking pictures, we didn't have to pass any parties. We handed off gear at the sixth pitch, (leaving Sickle), at the seventeenth pitch (King Swing), at the twenty-first pitch (Great Roof), and at the twenty-fifth and twenty-seventh pitches (Camps V and VI). At both the sixth and seventeenth pitch pendulums, we counter-weighted so that I was pulled up while Yuji was lowering. We used a Yates Rocker on the top of Dolt Tower, at the top of pitch 18, and on the last bolted anchor before the tree finish. These three places were chosen as places where I was simul-climbing on relatively hard terrain and Yuji was on relatively easy terrain. Any other combination would have called for short-fixing or "normal" simul-climbing.

We started at 7:15 A.M. It was a bit cold at the start, my hands barely staying warm enough to feel the pin scars on the first three pitches. After that, the temperatures were perfect. Upon reaching Sickle ledge, I checked the watch and a touch more than sixteen minutes had gone by since we began the route! That was almost three minutes faster than it had taken us on our attempt one week before. I've timed this route many times and Sickle ledge is almost always one-tenth the route time for a speed ascent. I was gasping for breath as we entered the Stovelegs at the seventh pitch. Luckily, I had a minute to rest there, as I waited for Yuji to get more than two pieces between us. The next check point was Camp 4, which marks the halfway point for speed ascents. We arrived at one hour and twenty-eight minutes! During the great roof pitch and all the top sections of the route, I was rapidly switching from simul-climbing to jugging to standard belaying to aid climbing, and back through them all. I managed to keep from going anaerobic, until the last 100 feet—where I pushed hard knowing I could collapse on top. Which I did, at 10:03 A.M.

We set the record at two hours, forty-eight minutes, and fifty-five seconds. This was terribly fun and rewarding. The Nose is my favorite route in the world. Covering so much beautiful granite in a pleasant morning was paradise.

We carried one #3 Camalot, one #2, two #1s, one 0.75, one 0.5, and doubles below that. We also carried six nuts, one cam hook, one etrier, seventeen quickdraws, eighteen free biners, six long runners, one Powergel each, one liter of water each, one ten-ounce can of UpTime drink, a Grigri, a couple of lockers, Petzl jugs, and a set of Yates Speedy Stirrups. We highly recommend this gear checklist for folks looking for a sub-five-hour tour of the greatest route on the planet!

CHAPTER 3
SPEED CLIMBING TIPS

Far better it is to dare the mighty things, to win glorious triumphs, even though checkered by failure, than to rank with those poor spirits who neither enjoy nor suffer much because they live in the grey twilight that knows not victory nor defeat.

—Theodore Roosevelt

Stick your neck out every once in awhile. It's good for the soul.

—Bill Wright, our translation!

This chapter is a collection of ideas for speeding things up. The tips are in no particular order, but they are grouped together under three headings: leading, aid climbing, and cleaning. I (H.F.) have given people some speed tips in the past and invariably they'll comment on one or two of my tips by saying, "That'll only save two minutes. What's the point?" The point is that if you save two minutes at every belay on a 30-pitch route, you've cut an hour off your time on the whole route.

That hour could mean the difference between topping out when it's still light or topping out in the dark, or topping out before the afternoon thunderstorms hit, or getting stranded on the wall while the storm rages. Simply put, if I give people four or five "two-minute tips" for every pitch on the Nose, that'll equal around five hours saved. Five hours saved translates into one less gallon of water to be hauled, four fewer energy bars to be carried, etc. The point is that each little speed technique you master adds up.

Tips for Leading

Stay in the lead. It is strategically better (in this context that means faster) to keep the same leader throughout the whole climb. But if you must switch, leading in blocks is better than switching every pitch. Keeping the same leader means she can recover from each pitch while waiting for you to follow. She gets used to racking the gear the way she likes, and you figure out how she likes it racked. I recommend, for the sake of speed, working out an agreement with your partner; for example, she can lead all of the Nose if you get to lead all of the Salathé.

Time limit for leader. Recently, Mark Melvin pointed out to me that you should consider giving each climber a set time to lead rather than dividing up pitches. Because speed climbing is about time, each climber should lead the same amount of time. So, one partner leads for three hours and the other leads for three hours. This seems like an equitable arrangement for non-speed climbing as well. Timing your leads makes you keenly aware of your pace on the route and can help tremendously when you need to consider important decisions like retreating or pushing on. It can also quell frustration between partners of different abilities and speed, in that neither will get stuck with more belay "duty."

We wrote earlier about the advantages of leading in blocks, so you might want to consider using blocks of time rather than pitches. Obviously, you shouldn't stop the leader in the middle of a pitch just because the clock runs out, but you can use the clock as a guide; change the lead where the terrain dictates within a general time frame.

Placing gear. When free climbing, try to place gear at your chest or below. This is a good practice to use whenever you climb, including sport climbing, and it is particularly relevant to speed climbing. The gear you place won't take up valuable handholds, plus you won't use extra effort placing the piece high. Why bring up that loop of slack to clip in? It is a wasted action.

The tendency to place gear above your head is motivated by security. With gear above your head, you are basically toproping. In speed climbing you are quickly above the piece you just placed (or the bolt you just clipped), so the advantage of clipping above your head is reduced almost immediately after placing it. Another reason for placing gear above your head is to postpone the next placement as long as possible. This is not as important when speed climbing because gear is usually placed farther apart.

Greg Murphy on a record ascent of the Shield. (Hans Florine)

Be smart about gear placement. Save pieces you will need up high. Burn a #1 cam if you have two of them rather than using your only #2. Think of fixed gear as a free extension of your rack. Use it liberally, but realize that this gear is suspect. Fixed gear has blown out on climbers, and you need to be aware of the consequences.

After running out a long section of moderate free climbing, don't clip into one fixed piece and start aiding. The consequences of this piece blowing out are huge. After a long runout, you need to place a solid piece, and one old copperhead is not going to do it. Once you've clipped a bomber piece, start using the fixed gear.

Favor using the fixed gear low on a lead or pitch when it is available. Higher on the pitch you can always use that cam as a draw or a cam, but draws can only be used as draws.

Your knot. Tie into the rope with the knot close to your waist, which makes it easy to keep your waist close to your high piece—an advantage when aid climbing. This also makes clipping ergonomically easier because you don't have to reach below your waist to grab the rope to clip. Once when I (B.W.) was on Astroman, I tied in with too much of a loop. For most of the climb, this wasn't a problem, but when I tried to follow the Harding Slot, the knot pulled up into the middle of my chest—the thickest part of my body. I was too wide to fit through the slot and ended up having to batman up outside the slot. I could have solved the problem by calling for slack so the knot would drop below my waist, but I was having problems making progress up this horribly tight passage.

Efficient movement. Certain climbing techniques are more efficient than others. When trying for speed, liebacking a crack may go faster than jamming it straight in. Liebacking is almost always quicker when ascending off-width sections. The disadvantage? It is much harder to place gear from a lieback position. Be conscious of other alternatives.

Tips for Aid Climbing

Etriers. Use four-step etriers instead of five-step. For about 95 percent of aid placements, you are *not* on the bottom step of your etrier. For the other five percent of the placements, just add a quickdraw to the etrier to get the length. Also, use light etriers. You don't want your feet getting comfortable. You want an incentive to move. Using different color etriers helps decipher what's what in the tangle. I use red for right and lemon for left. I designed a pair of etriers for Yates that are light *and*

Fear versus Speed
by Chris McNamara, Yosemite speed climber

The secret to taking two hours instead of six hours on a hard aid pitch rated A3-A5 is a matter of managing fear. The terrified climber makes slow, overly cautious movements, rarely gets higher than her third step, and often spends ten extra minutes trying to get the "perfect" placement when a fast and only slightly less secure piece would do the trick.

The speed climber, however, manages her fear and takes a much different approach. She gives each piece a solid bounce test, gets in her aiders, and marches right up to the second or top step. She realizes that once she has weighted a piece, she is committed, and there is no sense worrying about whether the piece will hold or not.

One trick she uses is to imagine that the piece, even if it appears marginal, is as bomber as a giant, ½-inch bolt, confidently telling herself, "This piece held for the last ten people, and there is no reason it is going to come out on me." Free of unnecessary fear, the movement up the pitch becomes fast, fluid, and much more fun.

Cam hooks. Become comfortable with cam hooks. Your first impression of a cam hook may be that there is no way in hell this thing will hold you. However, once you play around with them a little, you will find that these remarkable gadgets hold body weight in a variety of placements and save tons of time. On many pitches it is possible to put one cam hook on each aider and leapfrog them up long sections, saving hours of fiddling around with pitons or stoppers.

Miscellaneous Tips
1. Do not over-drive pitons.
2. To extend your reach another foot on hook placements, place the hook on top of your hammer and then slide it up the wall.
3. Create a mini-cheat stick by intertwining two stoppers together. This way you can extend your reach by one or two feet when trying to lasso rivets with no hangers.
4. Climb with lightweight biners such as the Black Diamond Neutrino or Kong Helium. This can take many pounds off a full aid rack.

comfortable. (Many climbers use aid ladders instead of or in addition to etriers. Nearly all of my comments are the same for aid ladders. We will use the term "etriers" for both.)

Some aid leaders use *two sets* of two etriers. One set is lighter and simpler, which usually translates into speed. On very difficult aid leads and continuously overhanging terrain, there might be an advantage to having two sets, though neither of us have ever used two, preferring to go light and simple. Another etrier tip: Once you've clipped the aider to the piece and bounce-tested it, immediately climb to the top or second step in your etriers. Don't waste time hanging out "down low."

Aid-to-free transition. Often A3 pitches have quick and easy 5.9 moves that can save you stacks of time if you're willing to get out of your etriers. I (H.F.) have seen too many 5.12 climbers waste ten minutes fiddling with a hook or placing a nut when they could have free climbed a 5.10 move in seconds. Get used to the idea of getting in and out of your etriers. Practice making frequent transitions from aid to free climbing and back again. Actually, you should practice transitioning from free climbing to French free climbing to crack jumaring to aid climbing . . . you get the point.

If you find it difficult to step out of your etriers and bring them with you at the same time, consider leaving them behind while you free climb a section. Once above the free section, place a solid piece, lower down to retrieve the etriers, and winch yourself back up to your high point by batmanning up the belayer's side of the rope. If you bring the etriers with you, be careful that you don't step on the trailing etriers. If aid climbing is over for the pitch, invest your time in balling up the etriers so they don't dangle down by your feet.

Wear climbing shoes. Wearing comfortable climbing shoes will always increase your speed, even if it's A5. You are *still* climbing. Don't settle into the mentality that you're just engineering your way up the wall standing in etriers. You should be constantly switching between aid and free climbing.

While I (B.W.) was climbing the Chouinard-Herbert on Sentinel Rock, my partner didn't bother to put on his climbing shoes because he thought he was only aid climbing or jugging that day. Later, on what should have been a trivial fourth-class lead, he found himself making some 5.5 moves. In his climbing shoes he would have made short work of this pitch; but without the confidence provided by good shoes, he spent more than an hour leading it. Wear your climbing shoes and keep the free climber's desire to move fast.

Pin scars. When encountering pin scars, consider hand-placing the pins rather than bashing them in with a hammer. Think of it as a hook move. Use a hook. Cam hooks are a godsend to speed climbers and frequently work great in pin scars. This not only saves time leading but also cleaning.

Use Black Diamond Peckers, A5 Beaks, Splitter Gear 2cams, and Pica Too-Cans like hooks in pin scars rather than pounding them in. Not only will they clean faster for the second, but the leader can easily pull these gadgets out and leapfrog them up a section. Previously, technology would require the leader to sew it up with pitons. Cams place and clean faster than nuts. When you have plenty of cams, use them before nuts even when there's a bomber V-slot.

Crack jumaring. When faced with a continuous crack, like on the headwall of the Salathé, clip a few of the appropriate pieces to the top of each etrier. Leapfrog the etriers up the crack, like a VersaClimber. You won't need to go back searching on your rack for the next piece. This is called crack jumaring (see Figure 3-1).

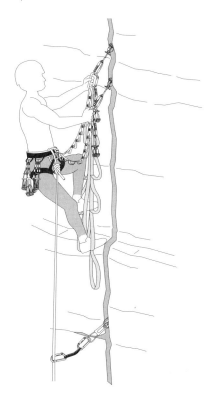

FIGURE 3-1

With a continuous crack, clip a couple of cams on your etriers and leapfrog them up the crack. This is called crack jumaring.

Crack jumaring is moving up a crack via etriers attached to pieces of protection. Usually the pieces of protection are camming units because they are easier to remove after being weighted. The piece is not placed and left behind but clipped directly to the etrier. Once you are standing on the top etrier, you slide up the bottom etrier to just below the top one, transfer your weight onto the bottom etrier, and move the top one up. Leapfrogging the etriers allows for greater movement with each placement but might be more awkward than the "inchworm" approach. Use what fits the situation best.

The motion is similar to climbing a fixed line, although in practice it takes longer and can only be done efficiently with very uniform cracks (and Yosemite is particularly rich in this category). Try to keep your foot applying a little downward pressure on the etrier while moving the unweighted etrier up like you were jugging a fixed line. This saves a tremendous amount of time with every movement of the etrier. If you had to replace your foot in the etrier each time, your speed would be cut in half.

Cleaning Tips

Racking gear. Rack gear on a sling as you clean, and rack the way the leader prefers so he doesn't have to re-rack it. Just hand off the sling to the leader when you reach the belay anchor.

Clip gear on the biner with a piece that's similar in size (one biner per piece is faster). This reduces the number of times you hand gear to your partner, allows for a quick inventory of your different cam sizes, and eliminates a horizontally expanding rack (see Figure 3-2). Also, clip two or three draws together so that you can hand off more than one at a time.

Saving energy. Wait until gear is at your chest or below to remove it from the rock. Your arms tire more quickly if they are above your head.

Ascenders. Even if briefly, try to hang in your harness from ascenders rather than on your arms when cleaning a piece. This gives you a minirest as well as two hands to fiddle with the gear. You will need to place ascenders above the pieces. Either unclip the piece or take the ascender off and move it above the piece. Practice taking ascenders on and off the rope with one hand.

Adjustable rack. If there is a big difference in height and size between you and your partner, it is worth having an adjustable gear sling, or a small one and a large one. If you use an adjustable gear sling, be sure it is quick to adjust and foolproof (i.e. won't ever come undone).

FIGURE 3-2

Grouped rack

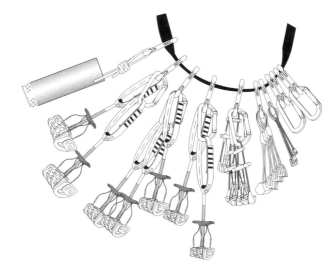

Horizontally
expanding rack

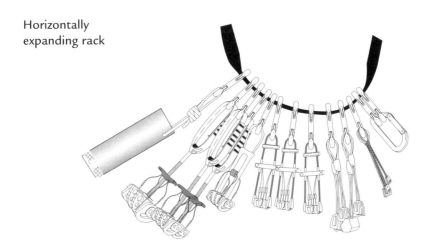

Cleaning draws. When cleaning draws off a bolt, unclip from the rope first, and then the bolt hanger, so the straight gate is in your hand and ready to place on the sling, rack, or harness. Slippery hands option: Unclip from the bolt; and while the bent gate is still clipped to rope, clip the straight gate to the sling, rack, or harness, then unclip the bent gate from rope. Both methods have the same number of hand movements.

Jugging. Practice ambidextrous jugging. If you are cleaning a traverse or diagonal pitch, it is easier to lead with the correct ascender. For example, lead with the left hand if the pitch goes left.

While jugging easy terrain on a traverse, like a third-class ledge, it is faster for the leader to belay you while you're on your ascenders than for you to slide your ascenders along. At the end of the traverse, the leader can re-fix the line and you can continue jugging.

Adjusting your etriers and jugging setup. Take the time to adjust your leg stirrups or etriers under your ascenders. If the angle of the climbing is steep, you want your feet a little closer to your ascenders. If your right leg is getting tired, lengthen your right etrier, and vice versa. I designed a leg loop for jugging for Yates called Speed Stirrups. It's a foot stirrup with an adjustable length. Metolius makes a similar item called an Easy Aider that works as well. Both eliminate the hassle of a bunch of aid ladder or etrier loops dangling around your feet while jugging. I went for years just tying a foot loop in a one-inch piece of webbing and using a clove hitch for adjustment—also better than an etrier for jugging.

Take the time to adjust the distance from your ascenders to your waist. As the angle of climbing gets steeper—and/or you get tired—you want to shorten this distance. This is only critical on the "lead ascender" because your waist will be on that ascender. The lower ascender tether should never be short enough to restrict movement.

Lower outs. If you know the route has big lower outs, bring leaver biners and a small lower-out line.

Pendulums. To keep from tripping, take your feet out of the etriers or jugging foot loops for big pendulums and lower outs. Forego the use of a hero loop or lower-out line if the pendulum swing is low-angle and you can control your swing by smearing, edging, or running. Be sure to check that the rope won't be rubbing on an edge.

Rope management. When there isn't any potential for the rope to snag, and especially if the pitch is straight up, I will tie in short once to have less rope weight on the brake end when belaying the next pitch, not as a safety back up. Obviously, if the wind is blowing the rope around and it might snag, or if the terrain is subject to snagging the rope, tie in a few times as needed. Time taken organizing the rope is better than going back down to unsnag it.

When you belay with a Grigri and then jug, leave the Grigri on the rope and pull the rope down through it. Eventually the rope weight will

Hans Florine and Chandlee Harrell on West Buttress record speed ascent. This is a difficult traversing pitch to follow. (Tom Evans)

be pulled through the device and you'll have automatic backup behind your ascenders. A Grigri is also useful for lowering out on traverses.

Cleaning a traverse. When cleaning a traverse, it saves time if you do not tie in short! People often recommend tying in short. I have never had a Petzl ascender fail on me. *People* fail to put ascenders on the rope correctly, but ascenders do not fail. Ascender accidents are due to improper use 99 percent of the time. Learn to place ascenders correctly on the rope—learn this well—and then tie in short if you must!

In regard to tying in short. In general, I will always have myself connected twice to the rock or rope system. For example, if I'm tied into the rope at an anchor, the rope is tied in with at least two knots, or I'm in with one knot and a daisy chain or sling. When transferring from one rope end to another, I might momentarily only be into the anchor with a sling or daisy.

When jugging a traverse, you've been weighting both ascenders for the length of the rope below you, so essentially you've been body-weight testing each ascender alternately. For a second or two, you remove one, lift it over a piece, and place it immediately back on the rope, as is the case on a traverse. You have just relied on *one* connection to the system for the time it took you to move that ascender over the piece.

Remember, the one connection you're on has been "tested" numerous times on the ascent up the rope to that point. This seems safer than what many folks do at belay anchors. I am always clipped or tied in to the end and/or the middle of the rope in addition to being clipped into the two ascenders. You should be too. So while jugging you're connected three times.

Satan's Minions Scrambling Club
By Bill Wright

From: Bill Wright
To: Scramblers
Sent: Monday, May 22, 2000; 1:28 P.M.
Subject: Angel's Way tomorrow!

Hi Climbers,
We're going to meet at the Devil's Thumb trailhead tomorrow at 5:30 A.M.—yes, 5:30. The plan is to run up Bear Canyon Trail to the Mesa Trail to Skunk Canyon. Then we'll solo Angel's Way (5.2 or easier). This is about a 1,000-foot climb. Then we'll continue cross-country up to the summit of Green Mountain and descend the Green Bear Trail to the Bear Canyon Trail and back to the cars. It will be about 2,700 vertical feet.

Bring sticky rubber approach shoes, a CamelBak, nerves of steel, tireless legs, and huge lungs. Should be a blast! (Once we get out of bed that is . . .) No one will be left behind, but know what you are getting into. Lots of running and lots of easy scrambling. We'll be in to work by 8:30 A.M.

From: Tim Nickles
To: Kevin Hamm
Sent: Monday, May 22, 2000; 2:20 P.M.
Subject: Angel's Way tomorrow!

Here's the e-mail describing that run/hike/scramble tomorrow morning. Basically, I think there is no way I am doing this.

From: Kevin Hamm
To: Tim Nickles
Sent: Monday, May 22, 2000; 2:54 P.M.
Subject: Angel's Way tomorrow!

Jesus Christ! This Bill Wright fellow sounds like one of Satan's minions. My advice to you is to avoid him at all costs.

Thus our little band of scramblers got our name. Henceforth we have been known as Satan's Minions Scrambling Club. We'd have early-morning "meetings" twice a week in the Flatirons above Boulder and have thousands of pitches of rock all to ourselves. We'd only see other people when we descended to the cars after the adventure.

The desire to mix trail running with climbing came from our competing interests in training for the Pikes Peak Marathon, climbing, and mixing training with busy work/family schedules. By meeting very early on weekday mornings we'd only sacrifice sleep. As Dennis Rodman says, "I'll sleep when I'm dead." But while we're still alive, we have things to get done.

Another motivating factor was the *Book of Armaments*, more commonly known as Gerry Roach's *Guide to Flatiron Climbs*. This charming, out-of-print guide lists a few hundred climbing routes, of which fifty-three are designated "classics." Roach then names the best of the best as the Top Ten. Hardly Manson and I did all ten in ten and a half hours in October 2001 when we found out that Buzz Burrell, local ultra-everything man, had done the routes in just more than fifteen hours. Bill Briggs later did the linkup in six and a half hours!

Most of Roach's routes are relatively moderate climbs in the third class to 5.5 range. This is a range where most club members are comfortable soloing the route in just a sticky rubber approach shoe. These shoes are a cross between climbing shoes and running shoes. We'd usually leave the car with only a CamelBak, but on tougher climbs we'd bring a rope and simul-climb the route.

The regulars consist of John "Homie" Prater, Mark "I Got Your White Rim Right Here!" Oveson, George "Trashman" Bell, Buzz Burrell, and many others. Once, we took Damon Lease, a visiting colleague, along. It was Damon's first experience with climbing and I suspect a rather unusual introduction. I can imagine the discussion that took place when he visited a more traditional climbing club back in Vermont:

Experienced Climber: We'll be heading out for a five-pitch 5.4 rock climb tomorrow, so be ready. I realize you've only climbed a few times before.

Damon: That's right. Just twice before. So, five pitches. Hmm, that will take about an hour, right?

Experienced Climber: An hour!? Clearly you don't have much experience. No, each pitch will take about thirty to forty minutes to climb.

Damon: Hmmm. That isn't how I've done it in the past. Why does it take so long? Do you place protection when you lead?

Experienced Climber: Of course we place protection! That's what the "5" in "5.4" means! Who'd you climb with before? Sounds like beginners who didn't know what they were doing. Good thing you didn't get killed. Now, remember to bring your hiking shoes tomorrow.

Damon: Hiking shoes? Aren't they difficult to run in?

Experienced Climber: Running? How'd we get on the subject of running? I said we're going climbing tomorrow. Are you listening?

Damon: I thought we ran into the climbs. I guess it's sort of steep on the approach, but don't you run out from the climbs?

Experienced Climber: No, we don't run. We hike in and out. You can't run while wearing a pack full of climbing gear.

Damon: What gear do we need besides a harness, rope, and maybe shoes?

Experienced Climber: Boy, you sure don't know much about climbing. You need your ten essentials, food, water, extra clothes, climbing rack, Figure 8, belay device, slings, prusiks, rappel gloves, headlamp, guidebook, etc. It's a lot of stuff. We'll be out most of the day.

Damon: Most of the day??!! I assumed if it was only five pitches that we'd be back in time for breakfast. My kid's got a soccer game at 9:00 A.M.

Experienced Climber: You thought we'd be done with climbing at 9:00 A.M.??!!

Damon: No, I thought we'd be done more like 7:30 A.M., but figured we had to run out and drive home. I assumed I'd be in the shower by 8:30 A.M.

Experienced Climber: Are we talking about the same sport?

Damon: Apparently not.

Experienced Climber: Who did you go climbing with before?

Damon: These Colorado guys. They even bitched about bringing a climbing rope with them. They told me to show up in my running gear.

Experienced Climber: See, that is a different sport. They were more like trail runners. That's not climbing.

Damon: Except that we did five- to ten-pitch 5.2 to 5.7 routes.

Experienced Climber: Hmmm, something isn't right here. I don't think we're communicating.

SMSC "disorganizes" a few "non-events" each year on the Flatirons above Boulder. To the casual observer these would look like races . . . maybe even to the not-so-casual observer. Our longest-running event is the Third Flatiron Time Trial. The time trial breaks up naturally into four sections: approach, East Face route (eight pitches of 5.2 climbing), rappel a fixed line, and run out. The total vertical gain is 1,600 feet and it covers about four total miles.

Looking at the Third Flatiron from Chautauqua Park, it is nearly inconceivable that the round-trip has been done in less than thirty-five minutes. This event started small, but it grows each year as others discover the joy of moving quickly and of competing. Is this a fringe event? Absolutely! But this is a fringe book as well.

You can view a complete report on this event and others by following the links on the Flatirons speed records page at www.wwwright.com/climbing/speed/flatirons.htm.

CHAPTER 4
SIMUL-CLIMBING

God has given me the ability. The rest is up to me.
Believe. Believe. Believe.

—Billy Mills, gold medalist in the 1964 Tokyo Olympics

Now we get into the weird and wild stuff of advanced speed. When I (B.W.) first heard of these techniques they seemed radical, but now that I've used them, they don't feel so strange. Simul-climbing is definitely different, but you might enjoy it. Are you ready for a new sensation?

Each route will present "obstacles" that require imaginative problem-solving. For example, when the leader is lowering out, preparing for a pendulum, the leader's weight may be used to pull up the follower as the leader lowers. Be willing to break with traditional techniques if you can increase speed without compromising safety.

Simul-soloing

On easy terrain, climbing unroped is an option that should be considered. Solo climbing is discussed in more detail in the next chapter. Simul-soloing is a variant of team climbing where you happen to be unroped.

You wouldn't rope up for a hiking approach, and simul-soloing is used on terrain somewhere between hiking and roped climbing. On blocky and loose terrain, often found on alpine routes, a rope can be more of a hindrance than a help. Dragging a rope along such terrain merely causes rockfall.

The simple fact of the matter is that big alpine routes have a considerable amount of terrain that is best covered with this technique. George Bell, Lou Lorber, and I were able to climb the East Ridge of Mt. Temple in a single fourteen-hour push, not so much because of prodigious speed (it's been climbed a lot faster!), but because we simul-soloed the lower 2,000 feet, which was Class 3 and 4 with some easy Class 5 climbing. The level of difficulty where this technique is applicable will vary with the party, but it should be considered for covering long stretches of easy ground.

Simul-climbing

Most of the time when you're simul-climbing, you're running it out a bit. You do this to conserve gear and because the terrain should be relatively moderate for you (otherwise you shouldn't be simul-climbing at all). The sole reason to simul-climb is so you and your partner can move at the same time. This is only valuable when climbing more than a single pitch, and simul-climbing frequently involves running many pitches together as one giant pitch. When Hans and Jim Herson set the speed record for the Regular Northwest Face of Half Dome, they simul-climbed the entire route and only restocked the leader with gear once—thereby turning a 24-pitch route into two pitches. Hence, you either have to run things out more than usual, or climb with a bigger rack than you normally would. In practice it is usually a combination of these two. If the climb has lots of fixed gear, your extra equipment can consist mostly of more slings and biners.

Simul-climbing is not safe. But you can certainly reduce the danger by holding fast to some rules. Rule Number One: The bottom person has to be 100 percent. He or she can *never* fall. I (H.F.) have suffered the consequences of a bottom-person fall. I survived and won't gamble like that again. I was simul-climbing with Andres Puhvel on the Salathé Wall. I was in the lead on the fourth pitch and 12 feet above my last piece of protection when Andres fell—he had pulled on a piece that failed. I was yanked immediately down to my last piece, which thankfully held. I suffered a bad rope burn on my leg and abrasions to my forearm and knee.

The bottom person can never fall! (See Figure 4-1.) When a leader falls onto solid protection with a good belay, the shock is cushioned by the dynamic lead rope. Not only does the rope stretch by 10 to 15 percent, but the belayer might let some rope slip and he might be moved upward as well. All this reduces the impact on the leader. But when a second falls while simul-climbing, the leader is pulled directly into the last piece of gear. If this piece holds, the leader will stop immediately, with no stretch in the rope—or anything else—to reduce the force. It will feel as if he had hit the ground. Of course, the forces can be so great as to cause the protection to fail as well.

If the leader falls during simul-climbing, the situation is not nearly as

FIGURE 4-1

Consequences of the second falling can be catastrophic. The bottom person MUST NOT FALL!

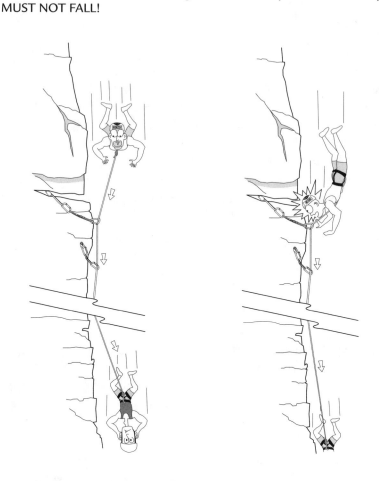

bad (though still not recommended). During Dean Potter and Timmy O'Neill's then-record ascent of the Nose (three hours and twenty-four minutes in October 2002), O'Neill fell while simul-climbing in the lead on the second pitch. Dean was jerked up the route a bit, he being much larger than Timmy, and his weight caught Timmy's fall. They then continued on, albeit a bit more carefully.

Imagine standing at the base of a route that pushes your limit. Would you solo it if the consequences of a fall were inflicted only on your partner and not you? Have you ever been out on a lead, way out on a lead, say 20 or more feet? You get sketched, and you visualize what the fall will

Who Leads While Simul-climbing?

1. Who wants to lead? Who wants the greater risk?

2. Is route finding a consideration? Who's the best route finder on the team? Does one of the team members have the route wired? If so, she should lead.

3. Who is fastest at placing solid protection?

4. Will one climber need a real belay on a few short sections? If so, it might be best if he were to climb second so he could climb on toprope with greater confidence and hence greater speed. On the other hand, leading this section might save a belay completely because the leader climbs with a pseudo-lead belay anyway (provided the gear he places is bomber).

5. Who is best at managing the rope? Who is best at climbing with one hand? The bottom climber has the very difficult job of rope management. She must never hold up the leader's progress, especially in a difficult section where the leader needs to move through swiftly. The follower also needs to keep the slack in the rope to a minimum in case of a lead fall, and be very diligent about not getting trailing loops of rope stuck.

be like. Maybe you have experienced such a fall. I've had a few such falls on steep sport routes and serious trad slabs—scary, but nothing compared to what would happen to you if you were 10 feet out while simul-climbing and your belayer jumped off the belay ledge, yanking you down to that last piece of pro. *Never* put yourself or your partners in a simul-climbing situation where the bottom person on the rope *might* fall.

Who's the leader? You might think the best climber leads, just like on a traditionally belayed climb at the crux pitch. After reading the last couple of paragraphs, you might reconsider and say, "No, the best climber needs to go second because he absolutely can't fall." The real answer is, like so much in life, it "depends."

Yes, it is absolutely catastrophic if the second climber falls while simul-climbing, but the truth of the matter is that no one should be falling. If the odds of a fall were more than 1 percent, I'd belay the pitch and not simul-climb. If one of the climbers is more experienced at route

Hans self-belaying on Zodiac; Jacqueline Florine (out of the picture) is cleaning the pitch; and Wayne Willoughby is organizing rope at the anchor. (Tom Evans)

finding and placing gear, it is frequently best to have him lead. The key thing to remember is that no one can fall. Having the best climber on the bottom does slightly decrease the chances of a catastrophic fall but might negate some of the advantages of a fast leader.

Another consideration is who wants to lead. Some people are very enamored with leading. The goal of most climbing should be to have fun, so pick the leader who maximizes your fun and speed. Climbing with a superb second is a dream. As long as the rack holds out, it is like leading on an extremely long rope, giving you the feeling of soloing the climb without nearly as much risk.

Hans has frequently been the bottom climber on speed records. His ability to manage the rope and his vast experience with simul-climbing make him a rock solid person to "anchor" the team. Choosing a leader depends a lot on the mentality of the climbers, the terrain being covered, and the risks each is willing to take.

The advantages of leading in blocks, mentioned in previous chapters, apply to simul-climbing as well. It is optimum to have the same person in the lead the whole time. This creates a cycle of rest and hard work that is not interrupted by a change in the leader. The exception to this would be when the follower can literally "swing" into the lead on a big pendulum. Hans and his fastest partners do this on the King Swing on the Nose.

Guides will almost always be the first on the rope, especially when route finding is an issue, which is a primary concern when hiring a guide. On moderate terrain, guides will simul-climb with strong clients whom they know well. Gaston Rébuffat climbed the North Face of the Dru with Réne Mallieux in such a manner. In fact, this climb provides a snapshot of the benefits and joys of climbing fast. Rébuffat describes the sensations vividly. "We had to climb fast, in fact very fast indeed, if I was to attend the guides' festival at Chamonix the next morning. This fact added zest to the whole day. To go fast merely for the sake of going fast usually seems senseless, but on this occasion it was quite different; we had only these few hours to climb the 2,500 feet of this face."

Rébuffat, like so many other climbers, had no particular love of just going fast, but once it was thrust upon him, he couldn't help but feel the joy. This experience has happened with us and the many friends we've introduced to speed climbing. They expect it to be a race, but it's not. It's moving with a sense of purpose and urgency and working together smoothly and not stopping and so much more. It is not missing out on what is great about climbing, but enjoying a new aspect of it.

Protecting the simul-climb. If you are simul-climbing and the lower partner runs into an unsuspected jam where she needs a belay, don't let it throw you. Put in a temporary anchor and use it to belay her until she is past her troubles, then resume simul-climbing.

You must have pieces between you and your partner that are equal to or better than a bomber belay anchor. Three bomber pieces are a minimum. If you do not adhere to this rule, you might as well both be soloing—and if you are soloing, do not do it tied to another person. This is not glacier-walking, where you and your partner have ice axes and can self-arrest.

Rope selection. Some people prefer a shorter rope, say 30 to 40 meters, so that the climbers stay closer together in order to communicate better. Sometimes a rope shorter than standard is not an option, such as when there is a rappel that is 25 meters or more. As the follower, I (H.F.) always prefer a Grigri to belay, so I tend to go for a 60-meter rope because the Grigri allows for a changeable rope length. (It is not correct to take your hand off the brake end of the rope when using a Grigri, *but* it frees your hands up for climbing! A safer alternative is to tie a figure eight on a bight below the Grigri.)

Rockers and Ropemans

Folks have used Yates Rockers and Petzl Ropemans to reduce the disastrous effects of the follower falling when simul-climbing. This is not an approved use of these devices. Some thought should go into their use. When using a Tibloc, be sure you put the rope *inside the carabiner* so the weight is not on the device alone in the event of a fall.

It should be noted, yet still not recommended, that a Petzl Microcender or a Gibs Ascender could also be used in this manner. Shortly after you place the ascender, it is advantageous to place a piece above it. (This is a good idea with the Rocker or Ropeman also.) That way a fall by the leader doesn't weight the device directly but rather the higher piece. The device just lets the rope slide until the follower catches the leader. I (H.F.) don't "endorse" this; I'm merely pointing out the best way to rig it. (See Figure 4-2).

I (B.W.) have tested follower falls with a Petzl Ropeman and found it to work quite well if rigged correctly, and if care is taken to prevent too much slack in the rope. Tiblocs, because they are not spring loaded, are not safe for use in this manner. These devices have stripped the sheath off the rope when used in this way, and are highly dependent on carabiner thickness and shape for solid contact with the rope.

Rope management. Do not simul-climb with huge loops of slack between you and your partner. This defeats the purpose of having a rope between you and your partner by greatly increasing the force of any fall. There are two ways to handle this problem. The first, less-than-ideal method is to have both climbers climb at the same speed all the time while on each end of the rope. This can be difficult and frustrating when one climber is on a tricky section and the other is on easy ground.

The second way to handle differences in speed is to have the bottom climber use a self-locking belay device like a Grigri. This allows the adept rope manager to throttle the lead line depending upon the demands of the leader and the speed of the follower. A drawback that inevitably arises from this method is that the loop of rope below the following climber can get stuck.

Communication. Good communication is always important, but even more so when simul-climbing. Make sure that you and your partner are

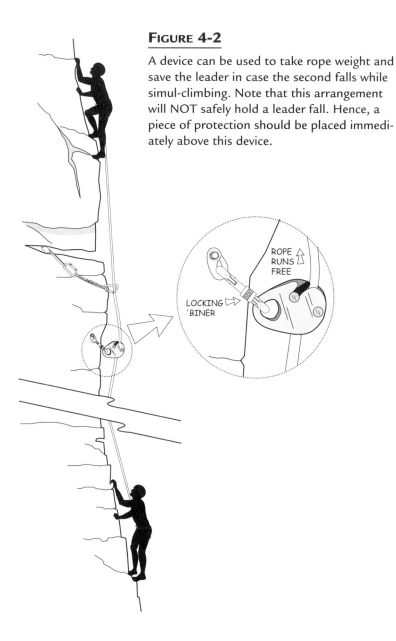

Figure 4-2

A device can be used to take rope weight and save the leader in case the second falls while simul-climbing. Note that this arrangement will NOT safely hold a leader fall. Hence, a piece of protection should be placed immediately above this device.

ROPE
RUNS
FREE

LOCKING
'BINER

aware of what the other is doing. I (B.W.) like to yell down "Placing a piece!" whenever I stop to put in gear. This lets my second know why the rope isn't moving. If he mistakenly thought I was at a difficult section, puzzling over the moves, he might become concerned and question why we were simul-climbing in the first place. In fact, I use this call whenever

Standard versus Speed Climbing: A Comparison

Speed climbing, paradoxically, does not necessarily involve physically climbing faster. By using special techniques to minimize the time you aren't actually climbing, you can ascend routes much faster not by moving faster, but by moving continuously.

Below is a graph of elevation versus time for two different climbs up the Yellow Spur in Eldorado Springs Canyon. The longer time line is of a conventional ascent I did with my friend Mark Oveson. We swung leads on the route, as a standard climbing party would. The extended periods where the graph is flat indicates where I'm belaying Mark as he follows the pitch below me and then leads the pitch above me. Notice that we do the seven-pitch route in a very reasonable time of four hours, including the approach.

The other line documents a speed ascent I did with Hans Florine. We simul-climbed the entire route as one pitch. Here there is no belay time, no change-over time, no setting-up-belay time, and no breaking-down-belay time. If we add up the time I was moving on the conventional ascent, we find it is roughly the same time as the simul-climbing time.

Both ascents were with great friends and were thoroughly enjoyable, but one of them I could easily do before work. One of these climbs I could squeeze in with only a couple of hours to spare before dark. One of these climbs could almost fit into a lunch hour.

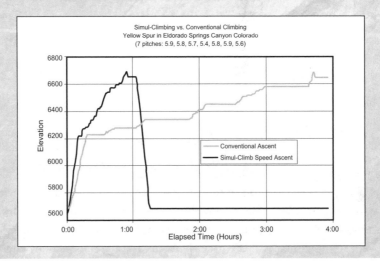

I'm climbing with my wife, Sheri. I don't want her to start worrying that I'm dragging her up a route that is hard for me and will be very hard for her. That's not why she climbs.

Another reason to inform your partner when placing gear is that it gives her an idea of how cautious you are being. On super easy ground, the follower might be comfortable with a piece every 50 feet; and on a more difficult section, she might be happier with solid gear every 20 feet.

Finally, it is important to shut up when there is nothing that needs to be said. When someone speaks, you want the other to pay attention. This is kind of "the boy who cried wolf" application.

Backing Off. When in doubt, the team must stop and belay. This is easy when the leader has the doubt, but may be tougher when the second is in doubt. Once I (B.W.) was climbing the West Face of El Capitan with Mark Hudon. He was leading and trying to link a 5.10d and a 5.9 pitch to Thanksgiving Ledge. I was simul-climbing below with the pack. I refused to climb the 5.10+ crux while simul-climbing and simply stopped climbing. Yes, this puts the leader in a serious situation, but it is much better for the leader to fall while down-climbing to a belay than for him to be pulled off by a falling second.

Simul-seconding

While simul-climbing might be a bit radical for some climbers, simul-seconding is a much safer technique that can really speed up teams of three climbers. To simul-second, it isn't the leader and the follower that are moving simultaneously, but both seconds that move together.

A traditional three-person team allows only one climber to move at a time. Hence, two-thirds of each climber's time is spent sitting at the belay. By simul-seconding, a three-person team can move as fast as a two-person team—plus offer the extra security of another member. Many people enjoy the camaraderie of climbing a pitch with their partner.

When simul-seconding, the leader must belay both seconds at the same time. This can be done either on a single line with both climbers tied to it, or by using two separate lines. Electing to lead on double or twin ropes is a natural in this situation and removes the dependency of the followers. Using a Petzl Reverso or similar self-locking device is recommended when top-belaying two people. If the terrain is moderate for the followers, it is not unreasonable for both of them to follow on the same line.

Deciding who will be on the bottom of a single rope when simul-

Bill Wright and John Prater simul-climbing on Chinaman's Peak, Canada.
(George I. Bell)

seconding is much simpler than deciding who will be the leader when simul-climbing. The best climber ties in to the end of the rope. I (B.W.) remember simul-seconding on one of my early morning scrambles. My partners and I would blast in to a slab route, climb it, and then run out in time to get to work before 8 A.M. One morning Homie and I brought along Damon, a beginner climber. I led the pitch, set up a belay, and called down to Homie, the more experienced partner, "Who's climbing up next?" We had previously agreed that Homie and Damon would simul-second the pitch to keep to our aggressive morning schedule. In his zeal to get climbing, Homie called up, "I'm going next." I tactfully responded, "Is that the best arrangement?" It only took a moment before Homie came to the same conclusion I had.

It was much more likely that Damon would fall off this pitch. If Damon were the bottom climber on the rope, his weight would come directly onto Homie's harness and pull him off. I'd be fine holding both climbers, as the belay was bomber, but it would be an unnecessarily unpleasant experience for Homie. The moral of the story is that the best climber always goes last when simul-seconding.

Short-fixing

The short-fixing technique is used only when the follower is going to jug the pitch. The leader pulls up all the slack upon arriving at an anchor and

The Carryover of Speed to Difficult Climbing
By Hans Florine

In the late 1990s, Chris Sharma and I went to Paris for the World Championships. This was before Chris was a world phenomenon—he made it into the finals and ended up taking second place!

As I sat and watched the finals, I set out to learn something about the way the best climbers approached the route to see if I could glean some pearls of wisdom to pass along— or better yet, to use myself. I decided to time how long it took each finalist to get to a certain spot on the route. I had done this at other events (but not kept detailed track of the results), so I had a hunch what to expect.

Sure enough, I was not surprised—without fail the competitors who most quickly reached the point I had arbitrarily marked on the wall got the highest on the route! In other words, those climbers who climbed the difficult route the fastest performed the best on that route. I saw Jean Baptiste Tribout, one of the most experienced competition climbers at the event, and Chris Sharma, with zero World Cup experience, *both* unlock the sequence to the route faster than other competitors. Both climbed higher than *all* others who took longer to get to the same place. Francois Petit won the event, and was one of the faster climbers as well.

My conclusion: Climb at a little bit faster pace on routes when you on-sight climb them. My reasoning is as follows: When you pressure yourself to *see the move quickly*, chances are you will see or find the move or sequence quicker. You will have spent less time on the route pumping out and more time *finding* the right way to go. Some climb faster because they can see a sequence faster than you—they have years of experience over you. Others might do a sequence that is a bit harder than necessary, but do it quickly just to get it done, rather than sit and pump out working to find *the* best way to get through a given crux area. Either of these reasons results in the same—you get farther along the route.

Thus, when practicing to improve your on-sight abilities and during an on-sight or competition performance, it is good to push yourself to go a little bit faster.

fixes the lead line so the follower can start jugging the rope. Meanwhile, the leader starts leading the next pitch with the extra slack in the rope— self-belaying until the second gets to the anchor. Once the second arrives, the leader is put on a standard belay, and he hauls up the gear cleaned by the second. This allows both climbers to be moving at the same time. Simultaneous movement is one of the key components of speed climbing, and climbing sure beats sitting at the belay.

This is particularly beneficial when the pitch being followed will take a long time to clean. It gives the leader something to do while waiting for the follower to clean. Even if you are climbing at a snail's pace when on self-belay, at least you're moving up. While your partner is cleaning 100 feet of nailed pins, even the slowest leader can get in a few feet of upward movement. When the follower arrives at the fixed anchor, you can pull up the gear on a tag line, or lower a loop of slack in the lead line to retrieve the gear from the last pitch.

There are many methods by which a leader can self-belay. She can use a device such as a Silent Partner or a Grigri, or just tie knots in the rope. If the climbing is easy and solid (free or aid climbing), the leader can even proceed without a belay, protected by just the loop of rope fixed to the belay.

Short-fixing is really the ultimate in two people moving efficiently. You can almost eliminate the "dead time" at belays where neither team member is moving up. In an ideal ascent where the short-fixing technique is used throughout the route, the leader will always construct an anchor before running too low on gear, and will continuously assess the gear that is remaining. If the leader knows she can only lead for another 20 feet before running out of gear, she will immediately put in an anchor and fix the rope so that she can continuing leading while the follower jugs up. If she runs out of gear, she's led too far before fixing.

Short-fixing is particularly useful at hanging belays, as these can be cramped and cumbersome locations. Getting just 5 feet up the next pitch greatly simplifies things when the second arrives. In this case, the second can just hand up the extra gear, but it is still worth it to avoid the gyrations of both climbers hanging in close quarters from the anchor.

With this technique it is even more strategic than normal to keep the same leader the whole time. If done correctly for the whole route, the two climbers will never be at the same place at the same time anywhere on the route. Wave goodbye at the start! This is exactly what Yuji Hirayama and Hans did on their record ascent of the Nose.

CHAPTER 5
SOLOING

Speed is safety!

—Mark Twight, extreme alpinist

In this chapter we cover speed climbing techniques as they apply to soloing. This is not a complete tutorial on solo climbing. You won't find too many instructors out there who teach roped soloing. Even John Long's book only has two paragraphs on this topic.

I (H.F.) have never had an instructor. I just went out and did some problem-solving. My first time out with a Silent Partner (a solo belay device), I actually had the rope clove hitched on the device improperly. I should have looked at the user manual more closely. The way I had it set up was safe, but the drag from the improper setup meant that it took five times the effort to feed out slack. I almost threw in the towel forty minutes into my seven-hour solo ascent of the Northwest Face Regular Route on Half Dome.

Traditional Roped Soloing

To make sure we're all on the same page, I will explain traditional roped soloing (see Figure 5-1). You, the soloist, start by building a bombproof multidirectional anchor and fixing one end of the rope to it. Next you attach a solo device to the rope, such as a Silent Partner or Grigri, and climb the pitch above, placing gear and clipping into the pieces. When you arrive at the next belay or anchor point, you build another anchor. Then you can rappel back down the rope to the first anchor, or down a second line that you trailed up with you. From the bottom anchor, you jug back to the top anchor, removing the gear as you go. (A second line is useful when cleaning an overhanging or traversing pitch.) Repeat this sequence until you top out. Basically, you ascend each section of rock twice, and rappel once. Fun, huh?

FIGURE 5-1

Traditional roped soloing

Lead   Rappel   Clean

This may seem laborious at first, but if you work out all the ways to be efficient about it, you can move at a good pace. This traditional method of roped soloing can be used to climb even large routes quickly. I used this method when I did my first solo: the Nose of El Cap in fourteen hours and eleven minutes!

Anchors. Get proficient at putting in anchors fast on any terrain. Make your anchors multidirectional or easily converted from a downward-pull to an upward-pull anchor.

Pitch length. In general, I try to go the whole rope length when I'm rope soloing, ignoring the standard belay anchors. Because you're never hanging at the anchor waiting for your partner to lead or follow, it doesn't matter if it's an uncomfortable hanging belay in the middle of a pitch or a comfy ledge. Setting up and taking down anchors is the most time-consuming aspect of soloing. It's always "dead time" because you aren't making upward progress. You want to reduce the number of times you have to do this.

There are reasons to stop on a big ledge. If you need a mental break or need to do some reorganization, a ledge might be just the thing. The gear on your rack also dictates your stopping point. You may have to stop before the end of the rope, and you don't have the option to simul-climb while soloing. However, you do carry the end of the rope with you, so you'll know when to stretch it that extra 10 feet and when to throw in an anchor 5 feet below.

Carrying gear. You want to move as efficiently as possible. When you are leading, don't carry anything you don't need. Weight kills your speed, and with the complexity of a solo system, reducing weight is extremely important. Gear that is useless on lead includes ascenders, backpack, wide gear (if it's a thin lead), extra water, and haul bag (if you've got one). You can bring all this stuff when you're on ascenders, going up the pitch the second time, or you can haul it up.

When rapping the pitch don't bring anything down with you that you don't need at the bottom anchor. You'll just have to carry it back up the pitch. You don't want to fight gravity any more than you have to. Leave the solo belay device, the rack of gear, and any remaining water at the top anchor when rapping down to clean the pitch.

Also, don't clean when you rappel! Clean on the way up. Why carry it down to the bottom anchor and back up? Some tricky pendulum traverses are exceptions. When you rappel a traverse, like the Great Roof Pitch on the Nose, you'll need to decide if you want to follow the line of the route when you jug or clean on the way down and do one big lower out at the bottom of the pitch. Different situations will dictate different answers.

Rappelling the pitch. If you are using a Grigri for soloing, it is probably also your lowering device. If you are using a solo belay device that is not convenient for descending, such as a Silent Partner, leave it at the top still rigged for leading so you can clip back into it and take off after you've cleaned the pitch (see Figure 5-2). Simply clip into the Silent Partner and unclip the knot labeled A. Using two carabiners at the anchor will make this fast and safe. This technique only works if you are at the end of the rope when you arrive at the anchor. And it will be a little tricky on natural pro when you're switching from an anchor set up for jugging to an anchor that may have to hold the upward pull of a lead fall. Use your judgment to find a way to quickly reconfigure the anchor so you can lead off of it.

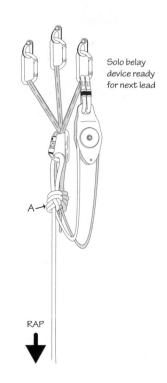

FIGURE 5-2

Rappelling the pitch

Solo belay device ready for next lead

A→

RAP

Traversing. Let's start with a scenario where you don't have a trail line (see Figure 5-3). If you're going to follow the line of the route on a traverse, lowering from the anchor (far right in diagram) and going left past each piece, try this trick: When you near the first piece, clip into it behind the rope with your daisy chain (frame 1); then lower enough so all your weight is on the daisy (frame 2). Next, unclip the rope from the piece (frame 3). Reclip the rope from the anchor into the piece above you and get your weight on the rap device (a Grigri is nice for this). Finally, unclip your daisy from the first piece and clip it into the next piece to the left (frame 4). Repeat this process at each piece.

If you have a trail line, the best way to tackle a traverse is different. Imagine a low-angle wall where the bottom anchor of a 200-foot pitch is only 20 feet right of the top anchor. If you clean on the way down, you have one easy swing out at the bottom, then it's just jugging a straight line back to the top anchor. If the same anchor setup was on a five-, ten-, or twenty-degree overhanging wall, I'd leave the pieces in and the rope clipped into them for the jug back up. It's easier and faster to jug on a

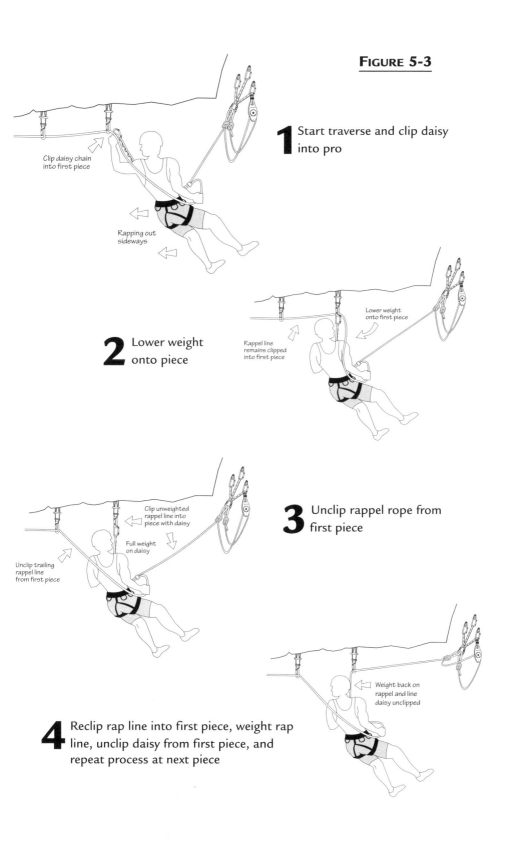

FIGURE 5-3

1 Start traverse and clip daisy into pro

Clip daisy chain into first piece

Rapping out sideways

2 Lower weight onto piece

Lower weight onto first piece

Rappel line remains clipped into first piece

3 Unclip rappel rope from first piece

Clip unweighted rappel line into piece with daisy

Full weight on daisy

Unclip trailing rappel line from first piece

4 Reclip rap line into first piece, weight rap line, unclip daisy from first piece, and repeat process at next piece

Weight back on rappel and line daisy unclipped

steep wall (when you can drive off the wall) than when you're dangling in the air 10 feet away from the wall.

Whenever there is a large pendulum, especially off an established anchor with a rap ring or leaver biner, consider lowering off it with all your stuff. Make the swing, build another anchor, and pull the rope. Cool! You don't have to backtrack that pendulum!

There are more things to consider in regard to traversing. More than I can address here—angle of the wall, sharpness of the traverse, and ability of the climber, to name a few. There are other ways to deal with a trail line. Use your imagination and apply some of the techniques discussed here. Each situation is unique. The idea is to make your efforts produce the most efficient and fastest way through the obstacle course.

Trail line tip. A trail line is useful for hauling and for emergency retreat, whether you're soloing or not. Here is a tip to consider if you don't have a partner. A Fifi hook can be used to facilitate solo hauling. When the pitch is straight up and down, set up the haul bag on the trail line with a Fifi hook so you can haul before you clean the pitch. If the haul bag gets stuck, you can free it when you go down to clean (see Figure 5-4).

Obviously, if you've led a traverse pitch, just rap the trail line, hook the bag to the bottom and lower it out, clean the pitch, and then haul. If you're not hauling, a trail line can be used as a backup and for jugging the pitch with a pack on.

Handling rope weight. When soloing, climbers complain about the rope weight they have to deal

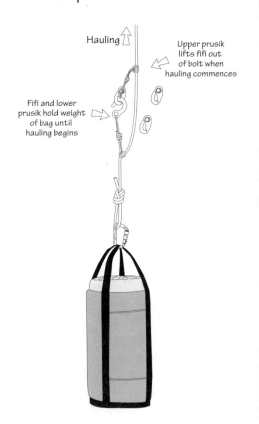

FIGURE 5-4

Trail line tip

Hauling

Upper prusik lifts fifi out of bolt when hauling commences

Fifi and lower prusik hold weight of bag until hauling begins

with. Knots on your pieces can be used to take rope weight and facilitate rappelling to clean (see Figure 5-5). Once or twice during a lead, I fix the rope to a good piece. (*NOTE:* This is not great when you fall because you don't make use of the full dynamic stretch of the rope.) Fixing the rope takes all the weight of the rope below that piece off of you. It can also keep the rope from abrading over edges both on the jug up and if you fall on lead. If you tie off occasionally, by the time you're on the last part of your solo lead, you'll have almost zero rope weight. Remember that when you solo, there is never any rope drag, so long runners are rarely needed. Compare this to a leader with a belayer who has nearly the entire weight of the rope and tons of rope drag at the end of a long lead! Now stop complaining.

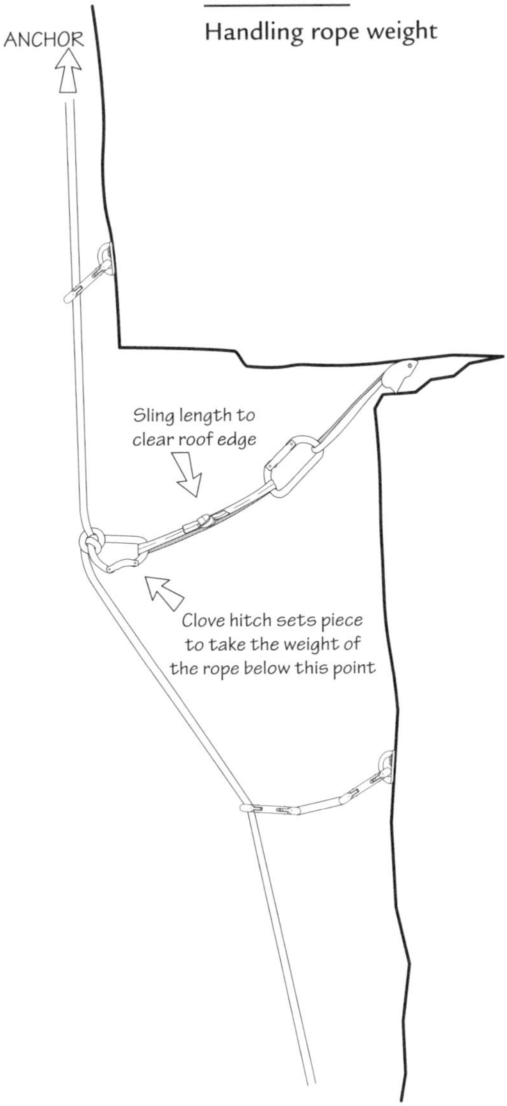

Rope management. Be careful with your rope management when you solo (see Figure 5-6). In normal lead climbing you are tied in to a single rope, but when you rope solo, there are at least two ropes—and usually three or more—trailing down from your waist. It can be confusing, and you have to get used to it. Different solo devices, such as the Silent Partner, will feed better or worse with less or more rope hanging from them. You'll learn the right amount for *you* with experimentation.

FIGURE 5-5

Handling rope weight

ANCHOR

Sling length to clear roof edge

Clove hitch sets piece to take the weight of the rope below this point

FIGURE 5-6

Be careful with your rope management when you solo!

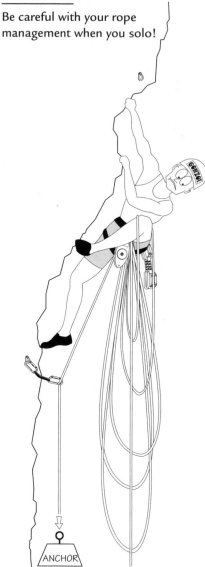

CONTROL

ANCHOR

With the Silent Partner, I usually have the rope tied in only at the halfway point when I leave the belay anchor. (Wren recommends backing up the device every 30 feet.) When I've led up half the length of the rope, I retie in so that there is about 20 feet at the end of the rope remaining, plus the new loop I've created. Some people restack their rope at each anchor in a rope bag and take it along with them. This is a great idea when the wind is bad and/or there are tons of flakes for the rope to get snagged or cut on.

Non-traditional use of rope when soloing. Just because you are soloing and you have a rope doesn't mean you have to use the rope in a traditional manner (see Figure 5-7). A few times, when there have been bomber rap rings, sturdy slings, or leaver biners, I've threaded through and "self-belayed" off of that piece or anchor. Then I have climbed along and not put in any pro. When I reached a safe anchor or built an anchor, I just pulled the rope as I would after a rappel. I didn't have to go back at all! Dean Potter used this technique when he soloed El Cap and Half Dome in a day.

You might rely on the two daisy chains you're connected to as your sole means of safety, basically "French free soloing." I (H.F.) protected myself on the 5.9 fist pitch above Dolt Tower on the Nose by clipping into my daisy chains, which were attached to a large camming device. Using this technique I was able to climb the pitch without dealing with my rope and, in turn, I set the then-solo record.

FIGURE 5-7

Non-traditional use of rope

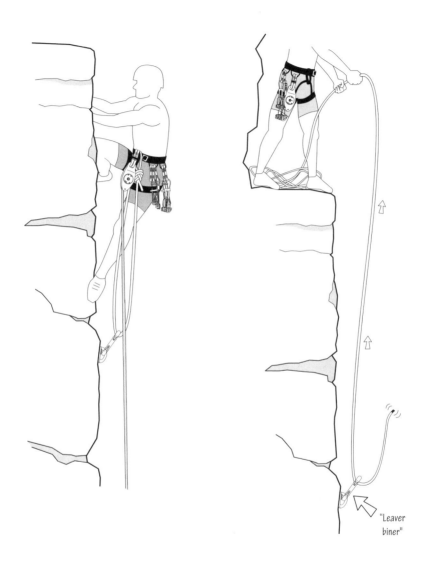

"Leaver biner"

You may occasionally loop the rope through a bomber fixed or "leaver" piece as you go by, then pull the rope when you reach the next fixed or leaver piece. This is a tenuous situation: Remember, you are relying on your pieces not to blow, or maybe even your handhold. Ask yourself, "If things fail, will falling back 10, 20, 30 feet or more to the leaver piece be an option?" On trade routes in Yosemite, the fixed pieces can be plentiful, but leaver biners could get expensive. (Obviously you could thread through slings as well.) Russell Mitrovich basically just French free soloed all of the Zodiac, or aid soloed on his daisy chains. The salutation of Greg Murphy strikes me here: "Go fast. Take chances."

Unroped Soloing

Bill and I both enjoy unroped climbing but do it at a level far below our on-sight ability (at least five number grades below for Bill, and usually more). Other climbers are quite comfortable closer to their limit. Derek Hersey, the legendary Colorado free soloist, would routinely free solo routes up to 5.11c when his on-sight ability was 5.12a—a difference of

only two letter grades. Hersey would on-sight solo up to 5.11a! Peter Croft regularly soloed routes up to 5.12a and Dean Potter once soloed a 5.13 sport route. Alex Huber has soloed a 1,500-foot overhanging 5.12 face in the Dolomites—and has soloed 5.14!

It seems that the best speed climbers can't help but be drawn toward unroped soloing. Nothing limits their speed. Some of the foremost soloists have also been the premier speed climbers. John Bachar, the first to envision and then climb El Capitan and Half Dome in the same day, is still legendary for his bold solos of up to 5.12c. Croft shocked the world with his amazing solos, including the first solo of Astroman. He also climbed El Capitan and

Bill Wright on the summit of Ancient Art, Fisher Towers, Utah. (George I. Bell)

Half Dome in a day with Bachar. Later, with Dave Schultz, Croft became part of the only team to climb both the Nose and the Salathé in a single day. Potter's bold extension of the speed climbing game was to combine unroped free soloing with speed ascents of the biggest walls.

Soloing is an individual decision, and it can be addicting. After soloing the Casual Route on the Diamond, Roger Briggs, noted Colorado speed climber, said he wouldn't do it anymore. He was afraid he'd like it too much. Derek Hersey, who once soloed three routes of 5.10 and 5.11 on the Diamond in a single day, fell to his death on the relatively easy Steck-Salathé in Yosemite. He was one of the world's best soloists and climbing on what was, to him, easy terrain. As they used to say on *Hill Street Blues*, "Let's be careful out there."

Unroped soloing is such a pleasant and unencumbered experience. All the bothers of gear, ropes, anchors, belaying, and rappelling are stripped away; all that's left is climbing. Bouldering shares this appeal, but most problems exist low enough to the ground to permit you to safely jump off a bouldering route. Soloing is a different story. Obviously, the climbing must be within your "no fall" range. People vary widely on the terrain they are willing to solo, and many great climbers won't even solo the most trivial climbs. The reward-to-risk ratio is not high enough to justify the venture for them.

I don't have any tips for going fast when soloing unroped. The simple fact that you are unroped is enough, no? One philosophical note: If you feel you *must* free solo fast, ask yourself, "Why am I doing this?"

Vision, Failure, and Triumph on El Capitan
by Steve Schneider

In California's Yosemite Park, there is a world-famous rock known as El Capitan. One of my first memories of El Cap is from a family vacation to Yosemite when I was eight years old. My oldest brother Bob was climbing a route on El Capitan; I tried to see him, but he was too far away. Then there was this big rescue for some guy on the Nose. I could see the rescuers lowering down the 1,000-meter face.

My mom was worried that it might have been my brother who had gotten hurt, but it also seemed like she was proud to be worried because, after all, that was her son climbing that huge wall. Not only did my brother come through unscathed, but he got to ride in the helicopter because he helped carry big ropes for the rescue. His motto for that climb was "Five days up, five minutes down."

I followed in my brother's footsteps and did the Nose eleven years later, having prepared by climbing several Yosemite big walls. The year was 1979. Four years prior the Nose had been climbed in a single day by legendary climbing figures. My partner, Stan Miller, and I remarked how phenomenal that was because we were climbing it in three and a half days. It seemed incredible to climb that fast. A few years later I came back and climbed the Nose with Karl McConachie in just more than ten hours. Through determination and effort, I had become one of Yosemite's fastest climbers.

For some reason I got it into my head that I had to solo the Nose in a day. Several big-name climbers had tried, but nobody even got close. It was one of the biggest prizes in the Valley, and I felt it was my destiny to accomplish this stunning feat. On my first attempt I failed, mostly because I could not find an efficient method to belay myself. Leaving the ground at midnight, I arrived more than twenty hours later at Camp VI—a descent ledge 600 feet from the top. I didn't have enough hours left on the twenty-four-hour clock to finish the climb.

Demoralized by my failure and completely exhausted physically and mentally, I decided to bivy. I never slept. The cold crept into my body, which caused me to shiver and my legs to cramp—it was altogether quite miserable. The next morning I thought about retreating but didn't want to quit what I had started. I summitted about thirty-seven hours after starting the climb, which sounded pretty good after I thought about it. It sure was hard to climb El Cap solo, but it was also extremely satisfying. It was the first climb I ever rope-soloed.

Some years went by and I forgot about the pain and suffering of the attempt. In the meantime, my friend Mark Blanchard, inspired by my attempt and a genius at metal work, made a self-belay device called the Silent Partner that promised efficiency and safety. I checked it out and decided to give the Nose another try. Nobody had soloed it in a day yet.

On my second attempt, everything worked great, especially the Silent Partner. I was at about the same fitness level as the previous time but made faster progress. The Nose is about 34 pitches in length, so I had to average about forty-two minutes a pitch. One strategy I employed was to start at 5 P.M. I would be rested and climb the first section with daylight. Then I would climb after dark while I was fresh and moving well. On my previous attempt I had learned that climbing at night was not much fun when you are exhausted.

On El Cap Tower, nearly halfway up the climb, I reasoned that I would probably make it if I did not get too dehydrated. Committing to go light and fast, I opted to carry less than one gallon of water. On Camp V, I got lucky and found some water—not a lot, but enough to make me comfortable.

The summit wasn't far ahead, and I still felt good. As I got closer, I got tired and excited at the same time. The prize of being the first person to solo the Nose in a day gave me new reserves of energy. I ended up with a time of 21:22:20. I measured from when I started climbing the first pitch to when I finished following the final pitch. I had done it—the prize was mine.

I really liked the feeling of digging deep within myself for more energy in the face of extreme fatigue. When I found that my inner strength was as strong as the task before it, I had a feeling of strength in my entire life. At the same time I thought about how big a climb it was for me and realized how small I was in the real world—next to the bulk of Mother Nature.

A few years later my best friend, Hans Florine, soloed the Nose in under fifteen hours. At first I was a little saddened that he had broken my record so convincingly. He looked at me with his pretty blue eyes and pointed out that we were the only two people in the world to have soloed the Nose in a day. That sounded like we were in an exclusive club of two, and I was happy again.

CHAPTER 6
THE ART OF PASSING

*Mind is everything; muscle—pieces of rubber. All
that I am, I am because of my mind.*

—Paavo Nurmi, winner of nine Olympic gold medals

What is the proper way to pass another team? I (H.F.) always figure the
team ahead has the power to say "yeah" or "nay." They have dibs on the
route because they got on it first. Whether you agree with this or not is
no matter. Always let the party you want to pass know that you are *asking*
them if you can pass. Simply by asking rather than demanding, you have
empowered them. They feel good about it, and everyone knows where
things stand. It's your job to be pleasant and seek permission to pass.
Setting up things this way has never failed me. It never hurts, and almost
always helps, to be nice, cheerful, and polite. Having the attitude that
you're going to pass no matter what is certainly not the way to start
things. Respect other climbers and don't give speed climbers, or yourself,
a bad name.

When you are coming up on a slow party, take a breather before you
reach them. Then climb confidently, in control, and quickly up to them.
By closing the gap on them fast, they are more likely to see how little you
would slow them down if they let you pass. Look for alternatives to the
route that would allow you to go around the other party without inhibit-
ing their climbing. Plan your breaks, if you take any, so that you can pass
in an easy place, like a huge ledge.

Choosing to pass a party that is at a belay anchor is obvious. Look at
where your ropes are and where they will be, then lead over, through, or
around accordingly. Passing people while they are on lead, or while one
member is at a higher belay anchor, may involve clipping into or over
their gear. Ask the other party if this is okay. If you don't ask, you might
spook the leader and cause them to fall *on you!* Always ask first!

Hans passes two Koreans just after King Swing. (Tom Evans)

I only clip another climber's gear if it is clipped to a fixed piece like a piton, and there is no chance of clipping through the fixed piece. If they have a 1-inch cam in the crack, I place another 1-inch piece next to it. There are too many bad things that can happen if you clip someone else's gear. Avoid it, not only for style and ethics, but for logistics and safety.

Consider imaginative solutions to passing. I went up the Zodiac recently and ran into a Spanish-speaking team from Basque. (*Mi Espanol es muy malo!*) Their leader was just finishing a long lead, and the cleaning was going to be time-consuming. I offered to clean their gear while I led, and then I had their second jug a free line. Instead of waiting for my follower to clean my lead, the Basque team let me borrow their gear for the next lead, and I hopped right to it. We fixed their line on the pitch above as a "trade" for letting us climb through. (Techniques like this work great but might invalidate a speed record. See Chapter 11.)

I've come across slower parties and handed them a Camalot or some biners or an etrier that they had left or that had gotten stuck a few pitches below. This surely bought me some goodwill, which made passing a lot easier. I've also fixed the rope on more than one occasion for people that let me pass. In the end, they got off the rock anywhere from thirty minutes to four hours faster.

Never use the argument that a party should let you pass because you are going for a speed record. Don't say, "I have no bivy gear" to get someone to let you pass, or whine that you are prepared to be out for only ten hours. The other climbers will just think you're pompous, or unprepared, or stupid.

A Hot Link
By Jim Herson (June 2001)

As they say, you just don't want to know how sausages, laws, and climbing plans are made. Our co-opted democratic system requires dopey pet projects to be funded by tossing pork at the other guy's dopey pet projects. Unfettered by fiscal reality, this system has worked just dandy and has given us such elegant documents as the U.S. tax code, among other gems. Climbing plans, on the other hand, are much more intricate. But the general principle of negotiating something utterly worthless and irrational by agreeing to something even sillier, while unconstrained by actual fitness, still applies. Thus, Peteman (Peter Coward) and I did a Salathé/Half Dome linkup.

The problem, of course, was Peter. What Tatjana sees in a man with such poor judgment of route quality is beyond me. That's right—Peteman didn't want to climb the Salathé! Weird, huh?

Borrowing a page straight out of Greg Murphy and Chan Harrell's playbook, I let Pete rant for a few weeks about just how done he was with the Salathé. Greg and Chan always let Pete, their "nocturnal specialist," carry on for the week before one of their trademark thirty-plus hour marathon climbs about just how done he was with the night shift. Only once his position is clearly stated will he happily cast off with the rack and headlamp. Pete and I have done the Salathé together three times and rapped in once in the last four years, so obviously I couldn't fault his Salathé fatigue. Instead, I just ignored him.

That isn't quite true. Pete and I had been toying with the idea of a jugless Nose/Half Dome linkup since Pete hates to jug and I don't know how to jug. So I played the linkup card to dupe him onto the Salathé. (Memo to self: Get fit before buying off partners with linkups.) Swapping a jugless Nose for the Salathé was trivial since as we all knew Pete ("the man who can't say no") was—how to put this delicately—a climbing slut. He loved climbing way too much to turn down the stone.

Of course, with a linkup the only goal is to be fast and efficient—two total non-starters for me. As this was probably my last shot at the Salathé that season I had no intention of passing up the best free climbing in the Valley. Much to Peter's dismay I was bent on doing some good, old-fashioned, anal-retentive, time-consuming redpointing. Unfortunately, Peteman is sharp and figured this one out all by himself. He placed a firm ten-hour cap on my free-climbing nonsense. Darn him!

As I enter my fifth decade, the infuriating Friday night traffic/late arrival/no sleep grind seems to have lost its luster. In fact, I refuse to fight it anymore. Instead, we enjoyed a casual ride up Saturday afternoon, arriving in plenty of time to cook a feast and make it to bed for a full six hours of infuriating insomnia. Arrg!

We started the Salathé at 5:15 A.M. and simul-climbed some to the crux, pitch 19, by 8:30 A.M. Knowing that we had another twenty hours of climbing ahead of us, I emptied the reserves trying to redpoint this pup, only to blow it once again at the last move. Arrg! I'm tempted to punt on linking the entire pitch and just go back to the original halfway anchors. Either that or I need a 4 mm cord since the rope drag at the top (130 feet out) is so irritating. Fortunately, the day was rescued a few pitches later when I (finally) redpointed the Teflon Corner. (Note: Due to the emotional baggage I didn't pack my magic shoes this trip).

My final goal was to give the Headwall a good go, but unfortunately after eight hours of climbing my arms called it a day. I needed a good hour's rest and I didn't have the heart to float the idea since that would definitely have been a non-starter for Peteman. I pulled through, and we topped out in the budgeted ten hours (B.W. Note: Jim redpointed the entire Salathé Wall via the nineteenth pitch (5.13c) in 2003, becoming the first person to do it this way.)

The turnaround from the top of El Cap to the base of Half Dome in full sun was, of course, the crux. The one-hour-and-fifteen-minute descent to the East Ledges wasn't bad and the major chow-down at the car was yummy. But the two-hour-and-ten-minute death slog up the slabs to Half Dome was hell. It was only my fury at the obsessive-compulsive case hiking next to me who wouldn't fold and call it a day that kept me going! (Memo to self: Find a partner who can just say no!)

At the base of Half Dome there were two way-too-peppy, in-a-day parties—although in our condition, Alan Greenspan would have seemed way too spunky. They weren't quite sure why we were starting Half Dome at 8:30 P.M., and we were too whipped to explain it. Anyway, let's just say Half Dome was slightly less fun and slightly less speedy than our previous ascent, but we slugged it out and topped out at 4:20 A.M. for a twenty-three-hour climbing day. On top, we tried to nap until sunrise but it was too cold. We made a slow, painful descent in our climbing shoes to the base, where we took a quick snooze, again got cold, and then hiked back to the car—a twenty-eight-hour, car-to-car-to-car day.

And then we committed the unthinkable: We headed home in daylight and recovered off company time! What were we thinking? And, although it's always tragic to rush the magical Salathé, I'll confess the sixty jugless, mostly free pitches were a kick.

CHAPTER 7
GEAR SELECTION AND RANDOM TIPS

In great attempts, it is glorious even to fail.
—Vincent Lombardi

How much gear do you bring? Is light right? In some cases, yes! If you've done a route before and you know what pieces you need, choosing the gear to bring is a cinch. Our friend, Greg Opland, has climbed the Mace, a classic Arizona desert tower, fifteen times. He has reduced his rack for this five-pitch route to just six pieces of gear by virtue of his experience on the route.

If you're strong on hand jams, you might consider *not* taking (or taking fewer) hand jam-size pieces, and the same logic goes for finger- or fist-size cracks. If you're making the rack for someone else to lead, consider their strengths and weaknesses. Remember, the more gear you take, the longer you can lead before having to stop and belay. Of course, more gear is more weight and that can lead to an unmanageable and detrimental amount at some point.

When you're climbing in an alpine environment, take a large selection of stoppers and hexes—rather than cams. The stoppers and hexes are lighter and cheaper, which is good if you have to leave them behind, as is often required in alpine adventures.

As with any leading, be imaginative about protection. Remember that a nut can be turned on its side to fit two sizes of cracks. A nut can also be used as a rivet hanger and a quickdraw.

Clothing

This is an extremely place-, speed-, and time-dependent subject. Choose your clothing based on where you are, your expected speed, and the time of year. In Yosemite you can go from shorts and no shirt to layers of fleece, a down jacket, and a water- and windproof shell over it all in the

A Cold Nose

By Jim Herson (January 20, 2002)

Darwin's mistake was in extrapolating from the complex finch to El Cap simpletons. Had he been a quiet observer in El Cap Meadows Sunday morning—forecast high of 43 degrees—he would have had to concede that the Kansas Board of Education had a point.

What he would have observed was two soft-bellied middle-aged yokels driving up in a family station wagon packed with multiple baby car seats and a sparse rack of cams. Being a sharp pair, the two bozos quickly noticed that Yosemite Valley was desolate—no sign of human habitation—that El Cap Meadows was covered in snow, and that the temperature was 24 degrees. At which point they both curled up into the fetal position and whimpered.

For the past three weeks I had been wheezing, hacking, and coughing nonstop. The preliminary self-diagnosis pegged it as Ebola/pneumonia, but as standard day care bugs go this was obviously much more serious than that. In addition to rendering the body utterly useless, the disease also shut down all rational mental facilities. Thus, Greg Murphy's frantic Friday night call suggesting we climb the Nose on one of the coldest days of the year, just because he hadn't climbed in the last two months, didn't strike me as all that unreasonable—other than the fact that it wasn't the Salathé.

Truth be told this was purely a scientific endeavor. Greg hypothesized that we'd be the only party on the Nose. I assured him that was a physical impossibility and that Warren Harding himself had to negotiate past a few parties.

The casual stroll to the base lacked Greggie's usual manic, psychotic flare, although our trademark haggling over what to pack was as fierce as ever. Captain Safety wanted to load us down with a second rope "just in case." I noted the importance of arranging the deck chairs on the Titanic. Of course Greg would sooner share his beer than defer to the All Knowing Beta Master. So we lugged the bail cord until we were safely hours behind schedule and then pitched it. I was firm on the big-ticket items though. To go fast and light—the days were short and a forced open bivy with Greggie seemed like a bad idea—we left the watch behind. This saved oodles of time bickering over that annoyingly ambiguous phrase "drop-dead turnaround time."

Being the cold-blooded venomous creatures that we are the first few pitches went down pitifully slowly. Then the sun hit and we started to thaw, as did the ice 3,000 feet up on the rim. We noted that perhaps the one helmet we had packed but left in the car would have been handy given the barrage of ice missiles whizzing by.

Despite the late and slow start, the warm sun made the forced open bivy less of a sure thing. Greg, however, was unwilling to chance a daylight descent. I painstakingly directed him into the Stovelegs, then turned away to have a hacking and wheezing fit, during which he managed to miss the most obvious and striking continuous straight-up crack system in all of Yosemite Valley. In his defense, Greg explained that he had only led this pitch six of the twelve times he'd done the route.

The midday thaw allowed for some outrageously crisp and surprisingly dry climbing. The Great Roof was the unexpected grand prize. The streaming green slim oozing out of the roof made slipping in those ultra thin marginal placements a breeze, not to mention cleaning them a total non-issue. And as though that wasn't enough, and no matter how cold and miserable the descent was sure to be, the tour de force was definitely slinging the icicle in the Great Roof! The Nose now goes at 5.9/C1/M7.

Swimming up the last few pitches in the dark was decidedly not the grand prize. We topped out with a good fifteen minutes to spare before the top pitches became frozen sheets of ice. The descent was no more treacherous than you'd expect snow- and verglas-covered steep rock to be, and took just slightly longer than my previous Nose ascent, which I had done with some blond yahoo.

And the deadly 2:00 A.M. drive home took on a surreal aspect, because it wasn't at all clear whether the dense Central Valley fog was inside or outside of our fried minds.

Gearing up for the Salathé Wall. (Tom Frost Collection)

same day. Ask the locals in the area what to wear—that's the best bet. The big thing to remember is that movement equals heat, and you're moving a lot, hopefully, when you're speed climbing.

Jacqueline Adams, Beth Rodden, and I were on a three-day outing on the Nose in March. For above the waist we brought T-shirts, light long-sleeve tops, a fleece jacket, and a shell. For below the waist we brought shorts and long fleece pants. One of us had shell pants. We froze our buns off! It was the coldest trip I've ever had up El Cap! When Peter Croft and I climbed the Nose on El Cap in a day in late spring, we both started with shorts and T-shirts. He threw off his shirt after the first pitch. We were plenty warm the whole way up!

FIGURE 7-1

Leader cloved into high piece and ready to take off.

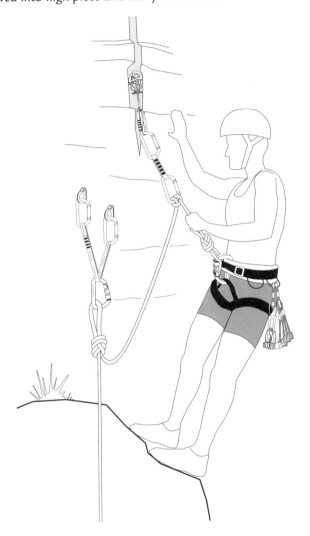

Random Tips

Clove hitch. Use a clove hitch (instead of a figure eight) to tie in to the anchor because it is easier to manipulate your hanging position. The clove hitch also tends to be easier to undo after it has been weighted. If you clove to the high piece at the anchor, you'll be ready to undo it and put yourself through it for the next lead, assuming you're leading the next pitch (see Figure 7-1).

Fixed gear. Call out when you've clipped a fixed nut or fixed cam. That way your partner won't waste too much time trying to remove it.

Partner's gear. Take a moment to familiarize yourself with your partner's gear before you climb.

Transferring gear. Do *not* take gear off yourself and clip it to the anchor, because then your partner has to grab it again and clip it to herself. Reduce duplication of work! Have your partner take it right off you and clip it where she wants, or hand the gear to your partner directly.

Approaches. When running or hiking on approaches or descents, clip the biners on your cams to the cam end of the unit so they don't swing around and hit you. On big cams there are usually biner-size holes on the camming section to clip to. On TCUs you can clip over the end cables between the end shaft and the trigger. For other cams, be creative and find ways to keep them from swinging around. Clip the biners on your quickdraws together to prevent excessive flopping.

One etrier. Consider using one etrier instead of two (or three or four). This keeps you thinking about free climbing or French free climbing.

Rope. Mark the halfway point in your rope. This saves untold time on rappels and in other situations.

Belay device. Always put your belay device in the same place on your harness or rack. That way you'll never have to search for it. The same goes for your nut cleaning tool and other regularly used items.

Rappelling. Consider simul-rapping when rap anchors are bombproof. With a 2- to 4-foot sling or daisy chain, clip your partner to the locking biner that also has your rappel device on it. Rap down the line in tandem with only one person attached directly to the rope. One advantage of tandem rapping is that the upper person can control the descent speed while the lower person detangles and deals with rope issues.

The other option is for both climbers to rap on opposite sides of the rope. Clip into your partner with a 3- to 5-foot sling or daisy chain. This keeps the climbers within reach of each other. I recommend using a block under the rap device in case either climber lets go of the brake end.

Consider lowering your partner rather than rappelling at the same time. The person being lowered can use both hands to flake or untangle the second rope as they are being lowered. This is much faster, especially if you are lowering down the route you just came up, and the climber being lowered has just received the toprope belay.

When rapping down a gully, or terrain where rope snags are possible, it is often better to rap twice with one full-length rope than to rap once with two full-length ropes tied together. If you have two ropes, have the first person down take the second rope with them and have them set up the second rappel while the second and/or third climbers are rapping the first line. When there are multiple rappels in a row, continue to "leapfrog" the ropes down to the bottom so that they can be used on the next rappel.

Partners. Climbing with different partners can introduce you to new (often faster) ways of doing things. You need to be discriminating about your partners, of course, but always be open to learning something. Make an effort to safely experiment with new methods.

Equalized anchors. If you're out of cordelettes or slings, simply tie in to each anchor piece with the rope. Leaving some slack between the anchor points allows you to make an equalized "master point," just as with a cordelette.

Night climbing. When night climbing, use a halogen bulb. You can lose a lot of time if you don't know where you are going. A good light will help you see features on the route. It's nice to have a dual headlamp—one with a regular bulb as well—so you can conserve battery power when you don't need to see past your immediate surroundings. There are now a variety of small LED headlamps to choose from, and many of them last for longer than a hundred hours. I highly recommend getting one. They're so small that there is no reason not to keep one in your pack or clipped on the back of your harness.

Linkups. Take time to plan ahead when considering linkups of multiple routes. Where will you leave your packs? How will you avoid excessive elevation gain and loss between routes. What are some of the sun/shade variables? Time spent on logistics beforehand can save you hours of extra work on the day of your linkup.

How-to books. Read a variety of "how-to" books. I like the manual put out by the American Mountain Guide Association (AMGA). Many basic systems can be illustrated well in a book. Simple tricks of the trade can be revolutionary to you, and me, when you discover how to apply them in some time-saving way. (*NOTE:* We are not AMGA guides.)

How-to videos. Existing aid climbing videos have good, useful information. Blend the information from the videos with tips in this book to make a hybrid system that works fast for you. I (H.F.) will have a "how-to" DVD available; check my web page—www.speedclimb.com—for short, free clips. I also recommend Alan Jolley's videos.

CHAPTER 8
FOOD AND WATER

If you're hungry, it's already too late to eat. If you're thirsty, it's already too late to drink. You won't die, of course, but your performance has already diminished, and that's important. This chapter stresses simple steps to proper fueling for a high output effort. Keep in mind that everyone's body responds differently to temperature and altitude. Also, your body will respond differently at different times in your life. There are many good books written about nutrition for sports performance.

When to Eat

If a route will take me less than two hours, I (H.F.) usually go light, with no food except for what is in my stomach. You can't carry all the food energy you'll need in your stomach if you're going for a twenty-four-hour push. I recommend many small meals during a long push rather than a few big meals. I try to eat a Power Gel or the equivalent (110 calories, twenty-eight grams of carbohydrates) every eighty minutes (I weigh 155 pounds). When it's really cold or you are sitting at a belay in chilly temperatures, you will need more energy to keep warm. When it's really warm or you are moving pretty fast and sweating, you will need to fuel that movement and replace the fluid loss.

I often eat when I am not hungry. I eat based on time, temperature, and movement. Sometimes I eat simply because I can, like when I am belaying a long lead or waiting for the follower to jug up. I try to never stop the upward movement of the team in order to eat.

I (B.W.) used to pride myself on how long I could go without eating. I'd go cragging all day long and never stop for lunch. My partners would always need to stop and refuel. While it is certainly nice to be able to draw on such resources, this is not the way to perform at your peak over a long period of time. If I had eaten more on these days, I would have had even more energy, climbed even better, and moved even faster. The primary reason I didn't eat was that I didn't want to stop climbing. Well, you can have both. The key is to eat on the approach, while belaying, and whenever you're not doing something else.

When I'm moving slowly, for instance on hard aid, I (H.F.) might eat less frequently. If I have just stuffed my face at the base of a route with a King Pin Apple Fritter, I might wait longer than an hour and a half before I start nibbling on my first minimeal. If I have less than an hour and a half of climbing left and I'm feeling strong, I might opt to not use blood supply for digesting the last minimeal, and save it for the top. When you eat, blood goes to your stomach and intestines to transport nutrients to the body and is taken away from the task of fueling muscle function—say in your forearms.

What to Eat

Variety is key. Choose a variety of things to eat for long pushes. When you get tired or are at high altitude, you often lose your appetite; and of course, this is the worst thing that can happen. You must eat so you don't bonk. If you bonk, your performance is diminished and it will take you longer to recover.

Give yourself every advantage by bringing a mixture of foods so that you increase your chances of finding something desirable. It's easy to bring along a few different foods so that eating is more pleasurable. Mix it up—try different flavors of energy bars and gel packets, and an assortment of trail snacks. Bring a bagel and maybe a yam, even an apple—although you don't get that much energy from an apple, they are wet, and more importantly, they are *different*!

For an eight-hour push on a 75-degree Yosemite day half in sun and half in shade, I would first be sure I had eaten well the night before and had a good breakfast. I would bring along two types of energy bar, two energy gel packets, a cup of dried fruit and nuts, and a small chunk of cheese. I'd also bring about two liters of water and hydrate really well before starting.

Water Is Life

Drinking after you cramp is futile. Plan on having the right amount of fluid and drink *before* you cramp up. And the right amount? Everyone is different. There is a minimum as far as liters per hour, but you must adjust the quantity of water to bring on a given climb based on temperature,

Peter Coward dying of thirst on Horse Chute. (Gregory Murphy)

movement, and availability of water on the route, the approach, and the descent. I take two liters of water for an eight-hour push.

I (H.F.) flavor my water with Champion Nutrition's Revenge, but any good sport drink will do. There are electrolytes and other stuff with big names in sport drinks that are good for performance. But just as important, your water should taste good so you drink more or more regularly. If you have an ongoing problem with cramping due to hydration problems, check for the potassium and sodium ratios in the drink mix you're using. Often, cheaper drinks do not have much potassium in them—and you may need more of that than plentiful (and cheap) sodium. Consider packing iodine tablets. They are small and light and can render water found on the route drinkable that otherwise is not.

Water Bag Versus Water Bottle

The best place to carry water is in your body, but for long hauls you must carry it somewhere else. The hydration systems by companies like Platypus, CamelBak, and Ultimate Direction are great inventions. Water bladders are typically carried in small packs with handy little pouches where you can put energy bars, headlamps, etc.

If you wear your water bladder during the ascent, you don't have to stop to drink. Frequently the effort to stop and pull a water bottle out of your pack is enough to make you put off drinking, thereby reducing performance. On multipitch routes you are often stopped at a belay waiting for your partner, so this advantage may not be a big deal, as you'll have time to pull out your water bottle. Certainly for soloists, the water bladders have a huge advantage.

Be careful with your water bladder in a chimney. More than once, I've pinched the tube of my water bladder in a chimney and had cold water flowing down my back. This might be refreshing in the Valley during the summer but very uncomfortable in the mountains during a fall ascent. If a water bladder breaks, and they do, you'll lose a lot of valuable water.

Water bottles have their advantages too. They are easier to dip in a stream and can be used to collect dribble from the wall. They are simple to clean, which is important if you've used a sports drink. They are easy to hand off between partners. If you are hauling, water bottles are more manageable. They come in a variety of small sizes—sixteen ounces, thirty-two ounces, etc. Compare this to the fifty- and one-hundred-ounce water bladders. I favor using crushable bottles so that you can gain space as the day goes on.

CHAPTER 9
TRAINING AND FITNESS LEVELS

*A fight is won or lost far away from witnesses—
behind the lines, in the gym, and out there on the
road, long before I dance under those lights.*

—Muhammad Ali

I (H.F.) could write fifty pages or more on details of specific workouts I've done to peak for competitions or to get ready for adventures such as hiking/running California's 14,000-foot peaks, but knowledge of how to work out is not the difficult part, finding the motivation to do so is the real challenge. I've read about many great training regimes, but they're all useless if you can't keep motivated. Still, I'll mention a few things . . .

The best training for climbing is climbing. If you're comfortable on 5.10, try pushing for speed on a 5.8 or below. You'll learn things on 5.8 routes that you can apply when you're speed climbing 5.6 to 5.12, or A0 to A5. Think about all the tips you've gathered from this book and apply them on a 5.8, not when you're pushing your free climbing limit on 5.12.

French Free

In order to French free quickly, you have to trust that your placements are bomber. The only way to gain this trust is through practice. Aid climbing is a great way to gain confidence in your gear placements. Because every placement is weighted, it is critically evaluated. If it fails, you're going to fall. While developing these skills, be sure to make placements very frequently to minimize the danger of a fall. Realize that cams rotate as you move past them; this does not render them unsafe. Experiment with this—cams often rotate right back into a "load-safe" position when the rope pulls down on them, as in a fall.

It is important to remember while French freeing that you are still "free" climbing. Yes, you are using aid and can't claim a free ascent, but view the piece as a natural hold and continue to use good climbing technique. Make sure you're putting your lead hip to the wall, using drop knees, and driving off good foot placements. Don't get sloppy with your feet just because you're pulling on a cam; that will wear you out in the long run.

Be very conscious of the direction you pull on a piece. Frequently pieces are not omnidirectional. Don't pull up on a stopper in a downward flare. A climber died on the first pitch of Beverly's Tower on the Cookie Cliff in Yosemite by grabbing a placement that was below him. Tragically, this was his only piece and when it pulled he took a fatal ground fall. There are two lessons here. First, never grab your only piece. If you're going to start pulling on gear, make sure you have at least two pieces placed. Second, be very aware of the direction of pull on your placements.

The ability to readily switch from aiding to French freeing to pure free climbing and back to aid climbing is a very valuable skill. It's not easy and takes practice, so work on it. Good routes for this are obviously ones that are a bit harder than your free climbing limit. Use aid on the sections that are too hard, use French free techniques for anything within a number grade of your on-sight ability, and free the other sections.

Non-climbing Training

It would be hard to think of any activity that would hurt your speed climbing. After all, "That which doesn't kill you makes you stronger." Swimming is great training. The motion and feel is very similar to speed climbing. If you're hoping to do a one-hour route, try to swim for an hour in the pool! Shoot, tell me that wouldn't make you strong. I'll point out motivation here again. If it's hard to get psyched for an hour of lap swimming, I'd suggest that you visualize the fun route you're training for while you swim. That way you'll get to enjoy the climb twice.

Lat pull-downs are a great climbing exercise. You can use less weight and do a ton more "pull-ups" than you might on a bar. Generally, I (H.F.) try to get in some pushing exercises as well when I'm in the weight room. This helps balance out the pulling muscles, which are constantly exercised while climbing. Climbers have overdeveloped pulling muscles, so seize every chance you get to beef up the pushing muscles. Do bench presses and triceps extensions. Working these pushing muscles in the weight room is a great way to reduce the chances of overuse injuries in climbing.

Fast-twitch Fibers

Studies have shown:

1. During a slow powerful movement, fast-twitch muscle fibers contribute to the motion more than slow-twitch muscle fibers.
2. During a fast powerful movement, slow-twitch fibers contribute almost zero to the motion.

My (H.F.'s) conclusion, assuming your performance goal is fast movement, is that when you train for particular motions either with weights or during other activities, you should exaggerate the speed of the motion to recruit fast-twitch fibers.

You can't take full advantage of the strength in your legs if your core is not strong enough to transfer that effort to your upper body. Core strength is paramount in all climbing. Work the lower back and those abdominal muscles. Find as many different core exercises as you can—there's plenty. Picture big man John Gill doing his front levers for inspiration, or my friend Phil Request, (6 foot 3 inches, weighing in regularly at 180 pounds) who can hold a front lever for 17.1 seconds. Do stomach crunches, use an ab roller, and do leg raises while you're watching TV. Hang on a bar or door jam and bring your knees to your chest. Lie on your stomach and do the Superman position, lifting your arms and legs up.

If it is available, check out the VersaClimber at the local gym. This is a climbing-specific treadmill. You should try climbing on the underside, as well as the topside. Basically you can simulate climbing a 5.4 scramble (on the topside of the machine), or a 5.10 jug haul (on the under side). You can train the climbing movement for a really long time without the need for a belayer! There are a few manufacturers of climbing treadmills out there—Brewer's Ledge is one of them. Find out if there's one at a gym near you.

Skate skiing is also excellent for developing speed climbing muscles. You're getting the arms pushing and pulling and the legs working in concert with the arms. If you use longer poles, you'll get a higher overhead pulling motion. Incidentally, tests show that Nordic skiers have stronger grip strength than any other athletes, including climbers!

Mile-high Mileage: A Full Day of Sport Climbing at Colorado's Shelf Road

by Mark Kroese, the author of Fifty Favorite Climbs *and a volunteer member of the Access Fund board of directors*

Nothing fuels my desire to climb like sitting in an all-day meeting—especially when it's with the Access Fund board. Because my fellow directors and I convene just four times per year, our meetings are long and tedious; we author climbing management plans, debate policy issues, approve grants, and review budgets. We talk about climbing, think about climbing, and study the impacts of climbing. We do everything, it seems, except actually go climbing.

After a February meeting, a group of us decided that come hell or high water, we were going to climb. We made plans to spend a day in Eldorado Canyon, just eight miles from the Access Fund offices in Boulder, Colorado. As luck would have it, the weather was perfect on meeting day, but the next morning greeted us with frigid temperatures and swirling snow. The closest warm rock was 150 miles to the south at a limestone crag called Shelf Road.

Undeterred, we piled into Chris Archer's Toyota 4Runner and hung on tight as he blasted down Interstate 25 while sipping a triple tall latte. Our foursome had more in common than our affiliation with the Access Fund. We all climbed at a similar level and, more importantly, we shared the desire to climb lots of pitches. We agreed that this was not a day for "project" climbing; we wanted mileage.

As Becky and Rob planned our itinerary, Chris assured me that each of us would lead ten pitches by the day's end. I reminded him that I had a 9:00 P.M. flight out of Denver International, which gave us about six hours to climb. "No problem amigo," he said with a confident smile. "We'll be super efficient."

And efficient we were. Before arriving at the crag, Rob reviewed the day's plan. "We'll start on the right side of the Cactus Cliff," he explained, pointing to the guidebook, "and we'll work left. This way, we'll do the harder routes first, and follow the path of the sun." Rob also suggested that we save hiking time by climbing at only one of

Shelf's many cliffs. We nodded in agreement, and as if breaking from a huddle, jumped out of the car and got to work.

Rob and Becky took the first leads, climbing 20 feet apart on neighboring routes. Within ten minutes both had clipped into the chains and were being lowered to the ground. As soon as Rob untied from the rope, I pulled it into the rope bag and he loosened his shoes. (We all chose to lead every route). I was on belay within sixty seconds and began pocket pulling my way to the anchors, clipping Rob's pre-placed quickdraws as I went. Instead of threading the rope through the chains and unclipping the quickdraws as Rob lowered me to the ground, I left the route equipped.

Sticking to our plan, we simply swapped routes with Chris and Becky. This way, only the first climber would need to place the quick draws, and only the fourth would have to floss the chains and remove them. The second and third climbers could simply clip, go, and lower. Our plan worked like a charm. After the first hour of climbing we'd each done three leads—a total of 12 pitches for the group.

We worked our way down the cliff with assembly-line efficiency, breaking for lunch after we'd done six climbs apiece. Because the last four routes were easier than the first six, we decided to climb in "blocks." Rather than follow a pattern of leading, belaying, then leading again, we would each lead two pitches in a row, and then belay twice in a row. This technique saves on transition time and builds endurance. After getting lowered to the ground, the leader stays tied into the rope (and in his shoes). The belayer pulls the rope through the anchors while the leader walks to the base of the next climb and scopes out the initial moves. Assuming adjacent routes, the leader spends less than a minute on the ground in between climbs.

Five hours after arriving at the base of the Cactus Cliff, we each completed our tenth route of the day. We all had wooden forearms, sore feet, and trashed fingertips, but the satisfaction of logging a thousand feet of limestone sport climbing made it all worthwhile. It was the perfect way to start the season. On the way home, Chris guzzled another triple latte, while the rest of us demonstrated how efficiently we could sleep.

Cardiovascular Training

The fastest climbers on long routes possess great cardiovascular fitness. Your workout should involve a lot of climbing—that's what we love to do, right? I (B.W.) like climbing in any form: running up a ridge, hiking a steep approach, biking uphill, etc. Running is one of the best ways to improve your cardio fitness, and trail running is the most fun. It requires greater agility than road running because of the varied terrain, and the varied movement helps prevent repetitive stress injuries. The softer surface of trails further reduces injury potential. Swimming and cross-country skiing are also great climbing exercises.

Running, skiing, and biking have all been used to enchain routes. If this is your game, then all the more reason to build your cardiovascular system. When Roger Briggs trained to break the record on the Longs Peak Triathlon—a human-powered trilogy that involved biking from Boulder to the trailhead (38 miles, 3,600 vertical feet), running to the base of the face (4 miles, 3,000 vertical feet), and climbing the Diamond (11 pitches, 5.10a/b)—he didn't train his climbing speed at all. He just worked on biking and trail running.

Motivation

"It is not enough to have the will to win. You have to have the will to prepare to win!" I (B.W.) forget who said it, but there are no truer words. When Santiago Botero was caught and passed by Lance Armstrong on a savage climb during the 2000 Tour de France, Botero knew that he had lost the race months before it started. Armstrong's smile said to him, "I was training while you were sleeping, Santiago. I won this race months ago when you were selecting which bike to ride. I was punishing myself in these mountains. I was preparing myself to win." To perform at your peak, you'll need to train. And training is hard.

The key is to find the motivation. It's great, and ideal, to work on your weaknesses, but if you can only get motivated to do what you're already good at, at least you're working out. Have fun—make it fun! Bill and I both wear MP3 players while running, climbing, and hiking solo. Put together a collection of inspirational music and visualize yourself smoking up a route in record time. Visualize, visualize, visualize! Think of cruising the Nose in six hours on a 70-degree day in June and casually getting back to the Valley floor and going for an ice cream by late afternoon! (This is what I do. Bill dreams of getting down in time for breakfast.)

CHAPTER 10
COMPETITIONS AND SPORT ROUTES

I love climbing precisely because it's pure play. Sure, sponsorships and sport climbing competitions have changed the equation (i.e. people are starting to train), but for things like big-wall speed climbing, it's still a bunch of friendly yahoos in pursuit of a worthless goal. It's nothing but fun.

—Jim Herson, holder of both the Salathé
and Half Dome speed records

Imagine clawing up a gently overhanging 60-foot wall as fast as you can using holds about the size of baseballs. A rival climber, only a body length to your side, is trying to claw faster than you on an identical route. To top it off there's an announcer blaring over a microphone and a thousand Gen-Xers screaming at you. It's similar to the crazy scene on the TV show *American Gladiators*, only Goliath isn't chasing you. Ah, the X Games experience! (The X Games dropped all climbing events in 2003. However, the World Cup tour still offers six or more events each year.)

There is not a standard wall for speed climbing competitions, and routes can be rated from 5.6 to 5.12 depending on the level of the competition and the organizer's particular goals. Speed climbers usually compete well below their top level. The route for the X Games was rated 5.9+, and the fastest time in 2000 was 11.54 seconds! The more experienced speed climbers made it look like swimming or sprinting rather than climbing. I (H.F.) usually set the speed route for local competitions at 5.5 so that 4-foot kids and 6-foot adults can compete on the same route. Sometimes the winning time is under five seconds.

Training for Competitions

As with any other endeavor, sport-specific training is the key to speed climbing. If you want to be a fast climber, practice climbing fast! After

World Cup 1992 in St. Polten, Austria. (Hans Florine)

you warm up on some very easy routes, pick a route that you're comfortable on and climb it at a faster than "normal" pace. In general you should speed climb a grade or two below your hardest ability. Look at the route again when you finish. Check out where you might skip holds or sequence your hands better to avoid extra movements that don't add to upward progress, like a drop knee. Often your butt is out from the wall quite a bit when you speed climb because you are driving your feet at a forty-five-degree angle to the wall. This makes your feet stick even if you don't hit a foothold.

Try to envision throwing the holds to the ground or swimming up the route without definitive stops and starts. If you can't move fluidly through the route, then get on something less difficult. Rest for two to six minutes and give it another go using the sequence you think is fastest. One sequence of holds will not be the fastest for every competitor. Find the sequence that works best for you. At most competitions you'll need to have the stamina to climb fast for four to ten races with one- to fifteen-minute rests between. If you can, find out the format for the event and mimic it in your training.

If you have aspirations of competing in World Cup speed competitions,

Tips for Competition

1. Practice on a route several grades below your limit.

2. Try *not* to look at your feet. Think of your feet as having a memory of where your hands just were.

3. Use imagery. Images are always a good learning technique. For instance, imagine swimming up the route or throwing the holds to the ground.

4. Generally, two short moves are faster than a strained long move.

5. If a competition allows, study how the other competitors are speeding up the route.

6. Try to drive off big holds with your legs. Think of pushing off the wall with your feet at a forty-five degree angle rather than pushing straight down. This makes your feet stick even if you miss a hold.

7. If you're competing and you can rehearse a route, practice the last 15 feet of the route more than any other part. Figure out the lowest point from which you can dyno for the bell.

8. Never, never give up! The other competitors may slip or fumble too. Go hard until you hit the bell.

you'll want to find a 60-foot wall. It is unlikely that you have one at your disposal, and few climbing gyms have 40-foot walls, let alone 60. Still, a gym is a great place to start regardless of the height. Climb a 5.9 jug haul on the longest wall you can find. Try different hand and foot sequences. Have someone start you off the ground with starting commands: "Ready, set, go!" For more information on all competitions, go to www.usclimbing .org and www.rockcomps.com.

If the competition allows, study how other competitors are speeding up the route. Focus on competitors who have the same body type, strengths, and weaknesses that you do. Take the best beta for each section from all the competitors and make a winning hybrid beta for yourself.

Here are some drills to practice. Try climbing a route fast and not looking below your chest. This forces your feet to remember where the holds are. The idea is not to stall your upward momentum by looking down. Next, try double-hand dynos up the route. For some sections of a

Tips for Sport Routes

Many folks can run to a local sport crag or climbing gym after work, and when you only have a short amount of time to get your climbing in, it is important to climb efficiently. Here are some tips:

1. Whether all climbers are leading or one or more is following, do not thread through the anchors until the last person in your party climbs. This has you belaying off the quickdraws until the last person lowers, which protects the fixed gear from excess wear and eliminates all but the last person from doing the thread operation. This should be the process regardless of the fixed gear: chains, carabiners, cold shuts, rap rings, etc.

2. When the anchors are two chains, do not clip into the bottom links because that is where you'll need to thread the rope after the last person in your party climbs.

3. Having a "cow's tail" or daisy chain on your harness can speed up your changeover at the anchor when you thread the rope. Quickdraws from the route you just cleaned work also.

4. Thread rope *behind* the draws or daisy that you are hanging on so that when you are weighting the rope for the lowering there is no tension on the biners for removal. Rappel only where very open cold shuts are used, otherwise wear from lowering is dangerous on the anchor (i.e. an anchor made of webbing). Never lower with the rope directly on webbing as heat from friction can melt completely through the webbing.

5. Think out the best sequence of climbers in your group to keep people climbing. For example, if you have three people, a simple rotation has each person climbing, belaying, and resting (which includes tying shoes and getting ready to climb). In other words, when the climber hits the ground, the person resting has his shoes on and is ready to tie into the rope for the next ascent. The belayer now becomes the person getting ready, and the climber goes to belay duty.

6. When someone who is not in your party is about to climb a route that you want to get on, offer use of your draws to them. When they are finished they can simply lower off, pull their rope, and waste none of your time going through the threading and cleaning process.

7. Many gym walls and sport climbs are shorter than 50 feet, which means a single 60-meter rope can be used to climb two routes that are close together.

climb, it may be faster to double dyno. Set up for the dyno by dropping low and hiking your feet high. Launch for the next hold and repeat rather than trying to climb smoothly through the section. Finally, practicing for pure speed is a great way to improve your climbing reflexes. Hold a friendly competition between some climbers at the gym.

Non-climbing Training

Because getting time in a gym isn't always convenient, include some cross-training activities in your workout, like swimming, rowing, and weightlifting. When I (H.F.) swim I try to freestyle sprint one length of the pool—which takes approximately the same time as it would to run up the speed wall at the X Games. Once you get strong, try this drill with swimmer's paddles so that your arms get more resistance. Finally, substitute leg thrusts for your flutter kick. Bring your knees up to your waist as if you were mimicking the leg drive of pushing off a hold on the climbing wall. This motion looks ridiculous—like you're trying to dog paddle really fast and failing miserably—but it is effective training.

If you're lucky enough to actually get into a scull and row, that's keen—but if all you have is a rowing machine at your local health club, that will work also. Always warm up, then try doing sprints at 80-, 90-, and 100-percent effort for ten to thirty seconds. Again, match the time it would take to go up a speed route. Rest for two to eight minutes in between sprints.

In the weight room, I try to mimic the sweeping motion your arm makes when you are climbing fast on the lat pull-down machine or a

The Principle of Applying Speed on Short Routes
by Hans Florine

In 1989 I had climbed only one 5.12. With my head held high, I went climbing at Stoney Point in Southern California. After warming up, I put a toprope on a 5.12 route. On this testpiece, on my first burn, I hung on the rope twice. After quite a struggle, I got to the top. This took me about ten or fifteen minutes.

From around the rock, my friend Andres Puhvel reared his head with a gleaming grin on his face. Andres had recently beaten me in a difficulty competition (by a hair) and had lost to me in a speed competition. Andres climbed at the same level as I did at the time. Maybe he had done one other 5.12. We had a friendly rivalry.

"Looks like a nice route," Andres said, "Do you mind if I try?" Reluctantly, I let him borrow the toprope on the route. He climbed it with no falls on his first try in about four or five minutes. "You looked very smooth," I said, gnashing my teeth. "It's really pretty simple," he said. Then he admitted to having done the route before. My jaw relaxed. He had done the route before so he had the beta.

"Hey Hans," said Andres with the smile on his face widening, "Let's see who can get up it faster." "Not interested," I said. "I haven't even climbed it yet. I can't even climb it slowly." I roped up for my second attempt and made it without falling. I didn't time it, but I'd guess it took about four minutes. Andres got on the route again and asked me to time him. He climbed the route in two minutes and twenty seconds! Then he proceeded to dare me to beat that.

I'm not one to back down on a dare, especially if it involves food or climbing, so I agreed. I didn't know whether I'd even make it without hanging on the rope. When the dust had settled, I'd climbed the route in one minute and fifty seconds!

Naturally, Andres could not let things stand and had to give it another go. He did it in one minute twenty seconds. On my next try, I did it in fifty-eight seconds! Andres went again and did it in fifty-two seconds! I thought, "Here's a route I couldn't even do three hours ago and now I'm racing up it in 58 seconds." It took me far less energy to do it in fifty-eight seconds than when I'd hung on it for ten minutes.

This experience brilliantly illustrated to me the importance of speed on short routes. Here's the moral of the story, kids: What I was doing the first time was "doubting" my way up the route. Later, I moved with decisiveness and confidence, and went through each move easily. To me, this was a significant revelation. Applying this observation to climbing made me start on-sight climbing at a little faster pace. My on-sight level went from 5.11d to 5.12c inside of ten months! I thought, "There's gotta be something to this speed thing."

My friendly rivalry with Andres did not end that day at Stoney Point. Andres called me a week later and said he'd climbed the route in 38 seconds! I grabbed my gear and got in the car.

similar device. This is good for keeping your arm speed up. Use light enough weight so that you can pull down as fast or faster than you would when speed climbing. Be careful when you do this because it's easy to slam the weights into the top of the weight machine.

Speed on Sport Routes

Many climbers scoff at speed climbing as an esoteric pursuit practiced by a small minority of competition climbers or big wall speed demons. But speed climbing methods and massive enchainments have been applied to short, one-pitch routes as well. In Joshua Tree National Monument, during the Yosemite off-season, John Bachar was infamous for soloing a "Half Dome Day" or an "El Cap Day." This involved linking together twenty to thirty routes in a single day so that the total vertical feet climbed equaled Half Dome or El Cap.

Linking routes together is quite natural for climbers with big appetites and only small local rocks. Just as the French started their enchainments of big alpine routes to simulate bigger mountains, the small crag climber can enchain many routes to simulate a much bigger cliff. Speed and endurance have also been applied to bouldering problems. A Web site called Birthday Challenge (www.birthdaychallenge.com) describes participants stringing together hundreds of bouldering problems in a single marathon day—among listing many other great challenges.

While speed is obviously necessary to climb as much as possible in a given time period, it can also be a key to successfully climbing difficult routes. A conscious attempt to speed climb may help you succeed on routes you've failed on before. How can you speed climb a route that you can't even climb at a relaxed pace? Speed can actually help you climb more efficiently by reducing technique-hindering inhibition and pessimism, which in turn lets your body do what it should be doing automatically and unconsciously.

George Bell on the Geronimo Finish of Deviate in Joshua Tree National Monument. (Photo by John Entriken; George Bell Collection)

CHAPTER 11
ETHICS AND STYLE

Badges? Badges? We don't need no stinkin' badges!

—Paraphrased from the movie *The Treasure of the Sierra Madre*

Rules for speed climbing? Rules?! Why not? We have specific rules for what constitutes a redpoint (though sport climbers have changed these over the last ten years). Why not specific rules for speed climbing ascents? To have a "record" for a route, certain standards must be followed. At the very least we need to ensure that the competitors are playing by the same rules.

Fixed Lines

In Yosemite, a set of informal rules has traditionally been used. While clipping fixed gear is allowed, using preplaced fixed ropes is not. Obviously, fixing ropes in advance would make the next day's ascent go faster, and lots of non-speed teams use this approach. It is common to fix ropes down from Sickle Ledge on the Nose and down from Heart Ledges on the Salathé. But on a speed ascent, the official start time is when the team first leaves the ground.

If the first time the team leaves the ground they are fixing lines and plan to return tomorrow, then the fixing day is the start time. This seems logical. Otherwise all speed records would degenerate into speed jugging contests up fixed lines. It might be speedy, but it's not speedy climbing. Spelunkers Chuck Henson (fifty years young) and Pat Smith both had a time of one hour and twelve minutes up El Cap on a fixed line strung right next to the Nose. So the record that Yuji Hirayama and I (H.F.) set of two hours and forty-eight minutes isn't *really* the fastest ascent of the Nose.

The ban on fixed lines isn't a new rule for Yosemite speed climbing. It was first established back in the Golden Age of Yosemite. An early reference to this ethic appears in Steve Roper's *Camp 4*. He recounts the first one-day ascent of the Northwest Face of Half Dome in 1966. He had "no thought whatsoever of fixing pitches the night before—that would have been cheating." Not only was this the first one-day ascent of Half Dome but also the first one-day ascent of a grade VI climb. Another grade VI climb would not be completed in a day until the Nose was done nine years later. It seems obvious that using someone else's fixed lines is a violation.

A controversy arose over both the fixed rope issue and consideration when passing other parties when Miles Smart reported his record solo of nine hours and fifteen minutes for the Zodiac. (The Zodiac is a very overhanging aid route on the southeast face of El Capitan.) This came just a week after Russ Mitrovich shocked the world by soloing this route without a rope in twelve hours—the first time an aid route of such length was done without a rope (see *Climbing* 190). The debate revolved around the fact that Miles Smart used another party's fixed lines to protect himself (he didn't weight the lines) and took a belay while passing a party (see *Climbing* 194). Smart originally didn't report these details and hence the uproar. As reported in *Climbing* 195, he claimed that using these techniques was "simple courtesy and sound mountaineering judgment" that allowed him "to pass them (the other party) quickly and efficiently, and avoid making them wait (while he led, rappelled, and cleaned to pass them)."

While this is true, and the other party probably appreciated his kindness, it does invalidate the record. Says who? Well, the climbing community in general. Most climbers consider Russ Mitrovich's ascent as the solo record on the Zodiac. Could Miles have gone faster and gotten the record on the route if the parties weren't there? Maybe. In the alpine world, using established fixed ropes is usually considered fair game. When Reinhold Messner and Peter Habeler climbed the Eiger North Face in a then-record ten hours, they used fixed lines that had been strung on the Difficult Crack by *The Eiger Sanction* film crew. The team freely admitted to using the ropes and didn't claim any speed record—though it was the fastest the face had been climbed to date. Alpine climbing is different than blitzing up the walls of Yosemite. In alpine climbing you do what's necessary to keep yourself alive.

Start and Finish Times

Is a committee required to certify speed records? Smart says, "Until Yosemite appoints its own version of the International Olympic Committee (IOC) to impose rules . . . the only fact that will never be

Hans on second variation pitch of Beggars Buttress (5.11). (Mark Kroese)

Timing a Technical Rock Climb

1. Start the stopwatch when the first person in your party starts climbing where a "normal party" would start climbing.

2. Stop the clock when the last person in your party and all the gear you're walking down with reaches the top, or the spot where a "normal party" would walk off.

Are there exceptions to these rules? Of course! I like to use a "car-to-car" time. This is easy enough to figure out. (Car-to-car times get complicated if you drive between enchained routes.) Bill, on the other hand, prefers a more specific starting location in order to eliminate the advantage of a good parking spot. For instance, the Half Dome Run starts at the sign indicating it is 8.2 miles to the summit.

disputable is the time you started on the Valley floor and the time you finished on El Cap's rim." In 1966, when Jim Madsen and Kim Schmitz were setting new standards for speed in Yosemite Valley, speed ascents were less rigorously timed. Instead of using hours and minutes, days and half days were used. As noted in Roper's book *Camp 4*, a somewhat jealous Royal Robbins stated, "Some climbers are extremely liberal in their interpretation of a 'half day.' It has a tendency to run up to 5 or 6 P.M." Like Smart's, some of the Madsen/Schmitz speed ascents were also tainted by the use of fixed lines.

Leaver Biners

What about leaver biners? Normally the rule is that all gear must be hauled to the top before the clock stops, and the implication is that gear will not be left behind regardless. However, leaver biners seem to be an accepted speed strategy. Let's take it to absurd levels for the sake of argument. What if a rich solo speed climber raced up a route with a couple of spare ropes and an unbelievable amount of gear, then left it all behind? This ridiculous example illustrates the difficulty in drawing the line between what is allowed and what is not.

Cache of Sorts

Another "style issue" involves stashing water, food, or gear along a route, or in between routes before you've started a single push ascent. Heck, Mark Overson once stashed a partner! He was doing a long traverse with one section that required a rope and a belay. He met his partner in the middle of the traverse, and also picked up gear, food, and water. Once the technical section was complete, he continued the traverse solo. Doing a "violation" like this is not grounds for excommunication from the climbing community—it's just important that you divulge the style in which you did the ascent. Why? So that if someone wants to "repeat da feat," they'll know how to plan their adventure.

Bottom Line

The bottom line is that almost no one cares about speed climbing, except the speed climbers. I (H.F.) will be the first to say that climbing is silly. To make rules about it is just piling ridiculous on top of silly. My biggest rule, if I were the "rule maker," would be that climbers must be honest about what they did. Then it is up to the climbing community to credit them with the glory, if any. You should be having fun. If you're not having fun, then make you're own rules so that you are. If outright lying or intentionally hiding crucial details about an ascent is fun for you, then I have no platform to talk to you, and personally, I'm not interested in your adventures.

I'm a firm believer that the power of competition drives humans to better their achievements. Competition is *healthy*! It is competition that has pushed the world's greatest athletes to achieve heights previously unimaginable. If we don't try to standardize how we're timing ourselves on routes, we can't compare our efforts. If we can't compare our efforts, we can't see if we're improving. The Brits call it "burning off your mates." The idea is to build on your mates' achievements. Hopefully this attitude is reciprocal and we'll motivate them to get off the sofa and try to best our effort. This continually supportive and competitive atmosphere improves everyone.

CHAPTER 12
THE HISTORY OF SPEED CLIMBING

Few places in the world are more dangerous than home. Fear not, therefore, to try the mountain passes. They will eliminate care, save you from deadly apathy, set you free, and call forth every faculty into vigorous, enthusiastic action.

—John Muir (1894)

For most of its illustrious history, climbing has been celebrated as a "non-competitive" sport. When the first speed climbing contests were taking place in eastern Europe, most of the climbing world frowned on such overt competition. Climbing, they thought, wasn't about speed—it was about ethics, difficulty, purity of line, and spirit. But climbing can be about speed, and there has always been competition in the climbing world. In some ways, it's just like running, biking, and skiing—no sooner were these sports being practiced than they were being measured by the clock. Like it or not, a climber's skill is often measured by how fast he does a route.

By most accounts, modern climbing started with Jacques Balmat and Michel Paccard's ascent of Mount Blanc in 1786. Climbing has since expanded from pure alpine into every modern facet of ascension, and speed has been introduced into each facet. In 1950 a client bet Hermann Buhl that he couldn't ascend and descend the Biancograt (north ridge) of the Piz Bernina from the Boval Hut in less than six hours. The climb involved 1,000 meters of climbing, and Buhl made it with not a minute to spare. Supposedly he descended 500 meters of steep snow on the very exposed ridge in only fifteen minutes.

In alpine climbing, speed is safety. This is a lesson continually being learned by climbers. Marc Twight, one of America's best alpine climbers, didn't learn this concept until he moved to Chamonix, at the base of Mount Blanc. In alpine climbing it is necessary to move fast while exposed to objective dangers such as cornices, seracs, rockfall, etc. In fact, crossing a glacier while roped up is the simplest form, and most commonly used application, of simul-climbing. It is standard procedure and no alpine climber thinks this is a radical technique. Simul-climbing on rock is more an expanding of the mind than of anything else.

In ice climbing, the same advantages of moving fast are frequently present. One of the boldest, longest, and most audacious ice climbs in the Canadian Rockies is Slipstream on Snow Dome. This route isn't the toughest, but it is a beautiful, continuous line that covers 3,000 vertical feet—a virtual El Cap of ice. You'd think such a route would be the most highly sought after route in the range, but it isn't: It is threatened by seracs and sometimes by a cornice and it is dangerous to spend too much time on this route. If you can't climb it fast, you really shouldn't be climbing it at all. That is, if you want to live.

A party of two climbing this route with standard belays may spend a long time in the danger zone. The first ascent took two days. In 1985, a team simul-climbed the route in five hours. Later, it was approached as a solo climb because of the danger involved and the relatively moderate difficulties (Grade IV+). The record time dropped to four hours, then three, and finally to Marc Twight's two hours and four minutes. Twight showed that, on a route like this, it was probably safer to solo the route fast than to climb it with belays. This isn't a valid option for most climbers, hence the route isn't climbed much.

The North Face of the Eiger

The North Face of the Eiger is one of the most infamous objectives in the climbing world, known prior to World War II as the "last great problem." Nine climbers died trying to ascend the face before it was successfully climbed in 1938. All of those who died were caught in bad weather, a major contributor to their deaths.

The Eiger rarely has good weather for many days in a row. In 1998 there was supposed to be a live TV ascent of the Eigerwand. The crew waited for good weather for forty-five days, and the ascent didn't occur until the next year. If you can climb the face in a single day, your chances of getting good weather greatly improve.

Warren Harding on the Nose in 1957, prior to the first ascent. (Allen Steck)

On August 14, 1974, Reinhold Messner and Peter Habeler climbed the North Face of the Eiger in a record ten hours. Later, Messner wrote: "I didn't climb the Eiger . . . to set any new record but in order to eliminate a large proportion of the danger." This alpine attitude of climbing fast would strongly influence Colorado and California climbers in the early 1960s. In fact, upon reading about Messner's Eiger ascent, Jim Bridwell made plans for a Yosemite response.

Yosemite

While speed climbing is practiced somewhat differently in climbing's sub-disciplines, it has been most visible in big wall climbing. When it comes to climbing big walls, there is no better place in the world than Yosemite—especially to push the limits of speed. The relatively benign climate and ease of rescue make Yosemite an ideal place to stick your neck out. I (B.W.) must hasten to add that I know of no speed climbing team that has been rescued from the walls of Yosemite, but certainly some unpleasant and unplanned bivies have occurred for overly ambitious climbers.

When speed first came to the big walls of Yosemite it was more because of style than anything else. Royal Robbins was the standard bearer for the Valley. He was interested in bold, hard, first ascents that pushed up the standards. Robbins didn't think much about speed, but he didn't ignore it either, because he knew it was a measure of competency. His second ascent of the Nose, with Tom Frost, Chuck Pratt, and Joe Fitschen, cut the time down from eighteen months to seven days. Of course, it is unfair to compare a second ascent to the first ascent because the first leaders had to place a number of bolts, and more so, had to overcome the psychological challenges of wondering if the route was possible.

Afterwards Robbins predicted, "The day will probably come when this climb [the Nose] will be done in five days, perhaps less." Robbins could hardly foresee that the Nose would someday be climbed in less than three hours!

When Steve Roper and Frank Sacherer ran up Steck-Salathé on Sentinel Rock in only eight and a half hours, Robbins immediately responded. Robbins and Fitschen had been the first party to climb the route in a day (and the only party up to the time of Roper's ascent). Robbins waited an entire day before heading up to Sentinel with Frost. For the first time simul-climbing techniques were used on a big wall in Yosemite. They did the route in three hours and fifteen minutes! But in general Robbins wasn't drawn to setting speed records; it was Roper who was attracted to such challenges.

Roper was one of the first Yosemite speed climbers. He was motivated by a desire to haul less and gain the respect of his peers. It simplified things if you could climb fast, because in the 1960s hauling was back-breaking work. Roper noticed that routes done over two days involved only fifteen to twenty hours of climbing. He figured you could "start early and climb a little faster, take less shit, and do it in twelve (hours)."

One-upmanship also began to play a bigger role, and route times were kept more meticulously. Roper confided, "A question asked more and more this year (1961) was 'How long did you take?' I was guilty of this, trying hard to make my mark doing what I was good at." Climbers didn't pursue records overtly, but anyone finishing a fearsome route in good style, which generally meant getting back down before the bar closed, was highly respected.

Roper was a naturally fast free climber and a very efficient aid climber. He became the first person to climb the classic 17-pitch Royal Arches route (5.7, A0) in Yosemite Valley in less than an hour—foreshadowing the current trend of car-to-car speed ascents of this route. His most significant achievement in speed climbing was the first one-day ascent with Jeff Foott of the Northwest Face on Half Dome in 1966—a coveted tick today. Roper recalls the ascent: "Sixteen long, long tiring hours, me starting the first pitch with hand-clutching the first hold, waiting for it to get light enough to leap upward. No such thing as headlamps in those days. And no thought whatsoever of fixing pitches the night before—that would have been cheating."

Even this early in the speed climbing game, there were rules. Some of today's speed climbing records, notably Miles Smart's time on the Zodiac, have been disregarded because of assistance. For a speed record to be valid the clock starts at the bottom and doesn't stop until you reach the top, and no form of assistance can be used along the way. These ethics originated with the Valley pioneers.

As fast as Roper was on the walls, he acknowledges that visiting Colorado climber Layton Kor was "super fast, far outdoing me." These two teamed with Glen Denny to make the third ascent of the Nose in three-and-a-half days—a time Robbins thought to be nearly impossible. Kor put up a number of first ascents in Yosemite, but also enjoyed romping up the classics – almost always at breakneck speed. In Gary Arce's *Defying Gravity—High Adventure on Yosemite's Walls,* Robbins said of Kor, "He never developed the ability to climb at any speed except flat out. He always seemed to be racing a storm to the summit." Jim Bridwell, part of the first team to climb El Cap in a day, called Kor "a climbing animal. You'd think he was on speed the way he raced up one route after another." Tom Frost, also quoted in *Defying Gravity,* recalled that Kor "didn't need any rest days. He didn't stop climbing until he ran out of partners!"

Kor's speed wasn't just due to his fast, efficient climbing. One of the

Bill Wright on the Salathé Headwall. (Photo by Tom Karpeichik/Bill Wright Collection)

biggest time sinks in climbing big routes are the changeovers at belays. Here, Kor was truly a master. He was probably the fastest changeover man in the history of climbing. More than one partner described being steam-rolled by Kor as he cleaned the previous pitch and swarmed through the belay, frequently stepping on his partners' heads, into the next lead.

According to Peter Haan, Schmitz and Madsen were the next team to push the speed limits in Yosemite. This team blazed up the walls in record times. They did the Dihedral Wall in "two and a half days." Their speed was so amazing that the old guard began to question them. A somewhat jealous Robbins was quoted in Steve Roper's *Camp 4:* "Some climbers are extremely liberal in their interpretation of a 'half day.' It has a tendency to run up to 5:00 or 6:00 P.M."

Sacherer was fast on the walls because he was fit; he was the best free climber in the Valley; and because he "rarely bothered to stop and place protection," according to Gary Arce. In fact, the ability to free climb is a key ingredient to climbing fast. Especially the ability to switch back and forth between the two styles and not get stuck either aiding free sections or trying too long to decipher a free move. Sacherer was mainly a free climbing pioneer, but he pulled off a number of first one-day ascents. His speed was mainly due to being able to free climb what others had to aid.

Haan himself, while no more of a real speed climber than anyone at this stage of the game, was quite fast on the rock. He attributed his speed to experience, but many of his best times were for roped solos where he wasn't burdened by a slower partner. Most climbers back then weren't consciously going for any records. As Haan put it:

> "It was kind of a 'feather' as we called it, to arrive back in camp with daylight left, after an important climb. It was all part of the 'flash' phenomenon: Could you 'flash' a route? Do it without hesitation, on-sight, easily, as a test of your mastery and depth? Mastery was how you were measured."

In an article for the 1972 *American Alpine Journal*, Haan wrote about his first solo of the Salathé Wall. He mused, " . . . All this damned hauling. If only one could just climb—climb without bags, water, packs, shoes, rurps, ropes, porters, maps, oxygen, and radios—merely as an incandescent unfettered being given to ascension, upwardness, climbing would not have the trembling impact it has."

The Nose and Beyond

By 1974, El Capitan had already been climbed in a day, but by the much easier and shorter West Face route. The Nose was the big prize, and the desire to climb this route in a single day led to speed climbing's biggest impact on the general climbing world.

In the spring of 1974, Ray Jardine traveled to Yosemite with Lou Dawson and Kris Walker and the world's only supply of a radical new device called a Friend. His goal was to climb the Nose in a single day. He first fixed ropes to Sickle Ledge, and tried for the top the next day. The team got pinned down by a storm around the Great Roof and were forced to bivy, but they had completed the first one-bivy ascent of the Nose.

The first one-day ascent wouldn't occur until the next year. Jim Bridwell wanted to make a statement about the superiority of American rock climbers and to this end he recruited John Long and Billy Westbay.

In line with their patriotic feelings, they planned the ascent for Memorial Day. Bridwell's team easily climbed the Nose In A Day, taking only fifteen hours. While this was only the second time a Grade VI climb had been done in a day, the ascent was a breakthrough for a number of other reasons. The route was broken into just three blocks and one climber led everything in that block before turning the lead over to the next climber. The climb also employed the three-man caterpillar technique to keep the leader moving as much as possible. This three-man technique would be the dominant speed climbing strategy for the next twenty years. Steve Gerberding, Scott Stowe, and Dave Bengston would use this technique to do many single-push ascents and bag the first one-day ascents of many of Yosemite's Grade VIs.

With the doors now open, speed climbing feats occurred regularly in the Valley and the evolution continued through the first solo of El Capitan and the first solo of the Nose. With solo ascents of the biggest routes being done in a day, the next step was obvious: multiple routes in a day.

The most notable was John Bachar and Peter Croft's 1986 climb of the Nose on El Capitan and the Regular Northwest Face on Half Dome in a day. In 1998 Florine and Steve Schneider became the first and only people to climb three El Cap routes in a single day. They did the Nose, Lurking Fear, and the West Face in twenty-three hours and thirty minutes. Croft and Dave Schultz are still the only ones to have climbed the Nose and the Salathé in a day. In June 2001 Jim Herson and Peter Coward climbed the Salathé and the Regular Northwest Face on Half Dome in twenty-three hours.

In the early 1990s speed climbing came into vogue and times started to drop on the trad routes. Steve Schneider and Hans Florine were major players in this movement, as they would be for the rest of the decade, but the star of the early years was Peter Croft. Croft's reputation was as a bold soloist. At the time he was considered the best free climber in the Valley and his solo linkups are still legendary. But the feat that left the climbing world totally in awe was his unroped solo of the 12-pitch, sustained, 5.11c Astroman in 1987. Croft climbed the route in about ninety minutes. This feat wasn't repeated until April of 2000 when Dean Potter, the current Dean of Speed, also soloed the route. Potter did the round-trip in 3.5 hours. Croft later took his speed and soloing ability to the high Sierra, completing monstrous mountain traverses.

Hans Florine, along with Steve Schneider, Miles Smart, Tim O'Neill,

Chris McNamara, Cedar Wright, Greg Murphy, Peter Coward, Chandlee Harrell, Jim Herson and Dean Potter, continues to push Yosemite speed climbing. Florine, an All American pole vaulter in college, has turned Yosemite's big walls into his own personal track meet.

In the late 1990s another speed climbing trend started; this time it was extremely competitive and resulted in the development of the latest speed climbing tricks. No longer could a record be obtained by simply moving efficiently and being very experienced on the route. The major players in this game were amongst the fastest in the world and everyone had these skills down cold. Now simul-climbing and short-fixing became much more prevalent. In the speed-soloing game new tools, such as the Silent Partner, were coupled with bold unroped soloing and leaver biners to set unprecedented times on the big walls.

In this latest movement, Dean Potter's nearly ropeless solo of the Regular North Face route on Half Dome was the signature climb. Dean, a phenomenal aerobic athlete who excelled at cross-country in high school, also started mixing approaches and descents with moderate climbs to create a new game of "car-to-car" times.

The challenge of doing routes quickly was not one of just climbing fast, but of problem-solving. Potter wanted a fast time on the Royal Arches, a 17-pitch classic route near Washington Column. The problem was the descent. The hike over to and down the regular descent—the North Dome Gully—was long and would be slow. Others had down-climbed the route to avoid this situation, but downclimbing was slow and there was the problem of reversing the pendulum on the route or downclimbing 5.9 friction. Potter discovered a shorter, albeit more technical descent, dubbed Potter's Gully, that allowed for a faster descent. The logistics of how best to put ascents and descents together intrigues some climbers. For some, the problem-solving process yielded speed ascents; for others, the task of working out time-saving logistics didn't necessarily make them speed climbers, but certainly shortened their climbing times.

Tim O'Neill applied his blazing speed to Cerro Torre. Climbing in Patagonia is purely an exercise in speed and endurance because of the small weather windows. The weather is so rarely good enough to allow climbing that when there is a good weather window climbers go nonstop and as fast as they can. Jim Bridwell used this strategy to make the second ascent of the Compressor route on Cerro Torre with Steve Brewer in only three days round-trip. This route took months of work over two years for Cesare Maestri to install the 350 bolts with his 160-pound air compressor. O'Neill and Nathan Martin climbed the route in only twenty-four hours. In 2002 Dean Potter soloed the route in 10.5 hours.

The next step was to link the big walls via solos. Dean Potter was the first to do El Cap and Half Dome solo in a single day in 1999. With Potter's feat unbeknownst to him, Hans Florine linked the same two routes, in reverse order, also in a day. The next year Florine was the first to solo two El Cap routes in a day when he linked Lurking Fear and the West Face of El Cap, setting records on both.

In 2000 Potter and Timmy O'Neill upped the ante once again. They started by simul-climbing the Regular Northwest Face on Half Dome, then descended the slabs to the Valley floor and biked (a completely human-powered day) to the Four Mile Trailhead. In an almost unbeliev-able time of two-and-a-half hours, they approached, simul-soloed (no rope), and descended the Steck-Salathé on Sentinel Rock—17 pitches of fearsome chimney climbing with a 5.10b crux section. After eating and another short bike ride, they climbed the Nose on El Cap, finishing at twenty-three hours and change. The next year, they replaced the Steck-Salathé with the South Face of Mount Watkins, thereby completing three Grade VI routes, all on different formations, in a single day.

The start of the 1990s marked the pervasive use of hard free climbing and simul-climbing as a means to speed. The three-person caterpillar style was still the favored speed method until about the mid-1990s. In 1994, Rolando Garibotti started making prevalent use of "short-fixing." This technique provided for the almost continual upward motion of a two-man team. Garibotti preferred this method because it was "so hard to find three partners willing to give 100 percent."

Garibotti, who'd later best Alex Lowe's time on the Grand Traverse, was not only very fast, but also very fit. He set records on a host of walls including Lurking Fear and the Shield, using the short-fixing technique. The method has been so successful that it has almost completely taken over the speed climbing scene.

As of late, the technique of soloing aid without the use of a rope has been used. The boldest example of this technique was Russ Mitrovitch's 1999 twelve-hour solo of the Zodiac. Mitrovich climbed the entire route sans rope (except for one 10-foot section) by using a system of three daisy chains that kept him clipped into at least two pieces of gear at all times. Nick Fowler has used this technique to set solo speed records on the West Face of the Leaning Tower and on Tangerine Trip on El Cap; the latter route is possibly the first on-sight solo one-day ascent of El Cap.

Colorado

While the big wall revolution was taking place in Yosemite, a lanky giant was rewriting the rules in Colorado. Layton Kor was racing up rock with such voracity that he literally wore out partners. Though he didn't realize it, he was Colorado's first speed climber. As has often been written, Kor only had one speed while climbing: fast. He was so full of energy and enthusiasm that he continually pushed the pace up the rock. He had no conscious thought about setting any speed records—he just wanted to get to the top. Kor was responsible for the countless first ascents in Colorado, many put up at breakneck speed.

In the late 1950s, the then-reigning king of Colorado climbing, Ray Northcutt, climbed the north face of Hallett Peak in Rocky Mountain National Park. News of this fearsome wall filtered back to the Yosemite big wall masters and two of them, Yvon Chouinard and Ken Weeks, made a trip out to Colorado to see just what these Rockies climbers were up to. They approached the 1,000-foot face in the early afternoon, planning to reconnoiter and then climb it the next day. Instead, they started up the face and just kept going, finishing in the evening. The second ascent of this wall took half the time as the first ascent. It wasn't due to familiarity with the face as neither climber had seen it before. It was just that they had superior technical skills and open minds. A mere 1,000-foot wall did not strike fear in the hearts of these Yosemite veterans. Half Dome was more than twice as high and steeper. El Cap was triple the height. A few years later Layton Kor would solo the route in ninety minutes.

One reason Kor was so fast was because of the era in which he lived. Free climbing wasn't a concern back then and Kor felt no obligation to work out the moves free. A lot of today's speed climbing is about letting go of the idea that pulling on gear is cheating. It isn't cheating, as it wasn't back in the early 1960s—it is just a different game. Kor naturally used whatever technique was fastest and, long before it had a name, he was a master at French freeing. Despite all the aid techniques, Kor was an excellent free climber, as evidenced by his numerous bold on-sight leads of blank face pitches in Eldorado Canyon. On terrain like that it was simply faster for him to run out the rope free than to stop and place a bolt.

Many of these terrifying leads were retrobolted afterward so that mortals could repeat them. The face climbing above the Psycho route in Eldorado is a classic example of this technique.

Kor was a voracious reader of climbing literature and worshiped the legendary Hermann Buhl. This Austrian climber was the world's preeminent mountaineer and when Kor read his book, *The Lonely Challenge,* he started solo climbing to emulate Buhl. The need for speed also had an impact on Kor, even though the motivations for speed in Buhl's alpine climbs were not present in Kor's crag climbing. Kor was famous for getting super early alpine starts for new ascents in Eldorado Canyon. Frequently these attempts would be stalled waiting in the car for enough daylight with which to see. With Royal Robbins, Kor would be the first to climb the Diamond in a single day.

Longs Peak

Longs Peak has been the site of many speed records. The earliest known record for attaining the summit from the trailhead was a pedestrian three hours: That was before Roger Briggs started whittling it down and promoting it among other speed climbers. Roger's first attempt took the time all the way down to one hour and thirty-eight minutes. The 5,000 foot ascent is almost completely a run/hike, but does involve 150 feet of 5.5 climbing up the North Face route. Briggs would eventually set a personal best of 1:24 before Chris Reveley, an accomplished climber and mountain runner, took the record with a time of 1:22. The current record is held by Mike Sullivan at 1:18.

A lot of the Colorado records seem to have evolved from the classic Longs Peak ascent and, hence, many Colorado speed records have been timed from trailhead to trailhead instead of the Yosemite method of timing technical climbs from bottom to top. This obviously adds a huge hiking fitness factor to the climbing difficulties, and enables mountain runners to compete for the record times. But not all records are accessible to runners.

The Diamond on the East Face of Longs Peak is one of the most famous alpine walls in North America. The Diamond itself actually forms the upper half and sheerest section of the East Face. Below the Diamond is an equally difficult, though less-steep face called the Diagonal Wall. Most ascents of the Diamond avoid the lower difficulties by climbing relatively easy chimney routes to the base of the upper wall. Nevertheless, the technical climbing is well over 1,200 feet. The record for climbing the Diamond from the trailhead is less well documented than that for climbing the face itself. Briggs has done a round-trip team ascent in nine hours, but that certainly isn't the record. The wall has been reportedly climbed in eighteen hours round-trip—in winter!

Another variation is climbing the Diamond from Boulder under human power (no official start site is known, but it is assumed to be in north Boulder near the intersection of Colorado Highway 36 and Broadway). This means biking the 38 miles and 4,600 vertical feet to the trailhead, then hiking in to the face and climbing the wall. Kevin Cooney and Neil Beidleman did the round-trip in an amazing ten and a half hours. But this ascent was supported in that they had a friend meet them with climbing gear at the base of the wall.

Briggs decided to clean up the ethics on this ascent, and after an entire summer of training that included mainly biking and hiking—and one solo of the Casual Route (5.10)—Briggs went entirely unsupported from Boulder to the summit of Longs via the Casual Route in an astounding five hours and forty-five minutes. Briggs climbed the Casual Route solo and unroped.

When Briggs first started climbing the Diamond, it was strictly an aid climb and always a two-day affair. But once the wall was climbed free, attitudes changed. Briggs discovered that by going light and climbing free as much as possible, he could climb the face in a single day. He figured his success rate went up about "one hundred times." Briggs has since climbed the Diamond more than anyone else—a total of more than eighty times, and growing every year. Once Briggs could do the Diamond in a day, he wanted to link up the Diagonal Wall as well. In 1980, with Kim Carrigan, he linked the Directagonal on the lower wall to the Complete Yellow Wall in fourteen hours, trailhead to trailhead. This wasn't the first time the entire wall was climbed in a day, though—that honor went to Jeff Achey and Leonard Coyne, who completed the Grey Pillar to the Casual Route linkup in the late 1970s. In the summer of 2003 Tommy Caldwell and Topher Donahue climbed five different routes on the Diamond in a single day.

Dean Potter, apparently not satisfied with dominating the Yosemite scene, visited Colorado and made a round-trip (trailhead to trailhead) ascent of the Diamond in four hours. This is a phenomenal time and the fastest known round-trip, but certainly well within reach of Briggs.

Assuming the biking in his Boulder to Longs effort took two hours and forty minutes (a very fast time) and the transition took five, Briggs made the trailhead to summit time in three hours. From there, Briggs had to run down the mountain in less than an hour. By removing the huge bike ride before, it certainly seems possible for a bold, fit soloist to post a sub-four-hour time.

Third Flatiron

Just as with the Royal Arch route in Yosemite, Colorado has speed climbing records for routes of modest difficulty—the most famous being the Third Flatiron, one of the world-famous and picturesque Flatirons that rise above Boulder. From easy scrambles to desperate sport routes, these rocks host countless climbs. The most famous of all these Dakota sandstone slabs is the Third Flatiron. "CU," standing for the University of Colorado at Boulder, is painted on this face in 40-foot-high letters. According to local guidebook author Richard Rossiter, the East Face of the Third is the "greatest beginner route on the planet." It is 8 pitches of 5.2 climbing on perfect rock, leading to an airy summit requiring three single-rope rappels to reach the ground.

Gerry Roach, a world-famous local mountain climber and Flatiron guidebook author himself, was the first to popularize a round-trip speed ascent of the Third. Starting from Chautauqua Park, Gerry got the round-trip in under an hour. Kevin Cooney did the round-trip from the CU campus—at least ten minutes away—in a similar time. Bill Briggs, Roger's brother, holds the current record for this fun, aerobic challenge, at thirty-six minutes and twenty-seven seconds, set way back in 1989!

Women Speed Climbers

The speed bug hasn't bitten the women as badly as it has men. In fact, Steph Davis, one of the world's leading female climbers, wrote a letter to the editor of *Climbing* magazine expressing disdain for the "childish efforts of one-upmanship" displayed by the Valley speed freaks. This is somewhat surprising since her husband, Dean Potter, was the Valley speed king. And Steph herself has been credited with a number of fast ascents in the Valley and around the world. The difference for her was the highly competitive environment that sought to shave a few more minutes off the record. She felt that didn't represent something worthwhile for the future of climbing.

Her argument is somewhat ridiculous if one puts climbing in the context of an athletic sport. Frequently climbers don't see themselves as pure athletes, but as adventurers. This is changing. Certainly with the World Cup climbing competitions, X Games speed climbing, and a growing number of bouldering competitions, at least some fraction of climbers views climbing as an athletic pursuit.

Probably the most accomplished female speed climber is Nancy Feagin. Feagin is an extremely well-rounded climber who participates in all aspects of climbing at a very high level. For her, climbing is mainly a matter of being a very good, very experienced, fit climber, and not using speed climbing "tricks." Nancy owns both the all-female (with Sue McDevitt in twenty-seven-plus hours) and the male/female (with Hans Florine in 12:30) speed records on the Salathé Wall.

Lynn Hill is the most accomplished and famous female rock climber in the world. For years she was the best competition climber in the world and became the first woman to redpoint 5.14. Once retired from competition, she turned to other activities. One of them was to free climb the Nose on El Capitan. As of late 2004, she is still the only person, male or female, who has led every pitch on the Nose free. What's more, she's done it in a single day! This is perhaps the most amazing speed climbing achievement in history, though she probably views it more as a free climbing achievement since she also owns the male/female speed record on this route (with Hans Florine in 8:40) as well.

The experienced Valley duo of Abby Watkins and Vera Wong held two of the most coveted speed climbing records in the Valley. They raced up the Nose in 16:30 and the Regular Northwest Face of Half Dome in 9:45. These records are now held by Heidi Wertz and Vera Shulte-Pelcum, and were set in June of 2004.

The Future

The jumps in speed, enchainments, unroped climbing, and 5.13 free climbing that characterized speed climbing developments in 1999 and 2000 were amazing, but these are now being taken to the more extreme ranges of the world. In June 2001 Steve House and Rolando Garibotti climbed Alaska's 9,000-foot Infinite Spur in just twenty-five continuous hours. The mixed line on the south face of Mount Foraker had seen only three repeats since its first ascent in 1977, and the fastest previous climb was seven days. House and Garibotti climbed with small packs and a single rope, and they simul-climbed most of the route. Dean Potter has soloed both Cerro Torre and Fitzroy (twice) in the span of two weeks. These climbers are taking speed techniques to the absolute limit, where the consequences of making a mistake would be huge.

In the crucible of Yosemite extreme free climbing skills are now required to set speed records. The speed records on the Salathé (Herson), Lurking Fear (Hirayama), Nose (Hirayama), Zodiac (Alexander and Thomas Huber), Leaning Tower (Leo Houlding), Washington Column (Matt Wilder), etc. are all owned by climbers who have freed or nearly freed these routes.

Speed climbing has at times been pursued very competitively and at times out of necessity, but perhaps it occurs most often just for pure fun. When Chris McNamara topped out after shattering the record on the Shield with Cedar Wright, he felt "one of the most incredible highs of my life." Duane Raleigh has written, "Once you get the taste for (speed climbing) . . . you're ruined . . . Speed gets your juices pumping." The ability to move quickly by cutting out extraneous gear provides a joyous sensation of unrestricted motion. Nowhere is this more exemplified than in the late Canadian climber Guy Edwards' nineteen-minute round-trip solo of the classic West Ridge of Pigeon Spire, where he stripped weight to the absolute minimum.

"I've soloed the West Ridge before, but I thought in order to achieve a sub-twenty-minute time, I needed to go as light as possible." Edwards said. "Soloing is about freedom; and soloing naked is a very liberating experience, kind of like skinny-dipping . . total ecstasy!"

Highlights and Speed Records

Speed breakthroughs are the big news in climbing, and following are the highlights of the past half-century.

1950: First one-day ascent of the Eiger North Face. Erich Waschak and Leo Forstenlechner climbed the 1938 Heckmair route in eighteen hours.

July 1959: John Day and Jim and Lou Whittaker climb Mount Rainier round-trip from Paradise (elevation gain about 9,000 feet) in 7:20 and spark an early competition for speed. Two weeks later, guides Dick McGowan and Gil Blinn make the trip in 6:40.

Summer 1961: Steve Roper reads Hermann Buhl and is prompted to make a mostly **unroped solo** of the Royal Arches route (5.7, A0) in less than an hour. This same style of mostly unroped soloing would be applied by Dean Potter thirty-seven years later on the Regular Northwest Face of Half Dome (5.12b, A0).

1961: Claudio Barbier links up all five north faces of the Tre Cime di Lavaredo in the Dolomites in a single day—one of the first big **enchainments.** This is the vertical equivalent of El Capitan and Half Dome.

September 1961: Steve Roper and Frank Sacherer on-sight the Steck-Salathé in 8:30. This is the first one-day on-sight of a Grade V route.

September 1961: Royal Robbins and Tom Frost climb the Steck-Salathé in 3:15, introducing **simul-climbing** techniques and **overtly competitive** speed climbing to the Valley.

July 13, 1963: Layton Kor and Royal Robbins make the first one-day ascent of the Diamond on Longs Peak.

Summer 1964: Federick Morshead climbs Mont Blanc from Chamonix—a vertical gain of 3,600 meters—in a round-trip time of 16.5 hours.

May 1966: Steve Roper and Jeff Foott climb the Regular Northwest Face of Half Dome in a day. This is the first one-day ascent of a Grade VI route. They establish the rule of **no fixed lines** for a one-day ascent.

July 19, 1969: Reinhold Messner solos the North Face of Les Droites, the route's first one-day ascent.

Spring 1974: Ray Jardine, along with Lou Dawson and Kris Walker, climb the Nose of El Cap in twenty-eight hours spread over three days. Their extraordinary speed was partially due to using the world's only supply of **Friends.** Jardine had "invented Friends specifically with a speed climb of the Nose in mind."

1974: The "Climbing Smiths" (father George Smith and sons Flint, Quade, Cody, and Tyle) climbed all fifty-four of Colorado Fourteeners in thirty-three days, and then continued on to California and Washington to climb sixty-eight 14,000-plus-foot mountains in the lower forty-eight states in a still-standing record of forty-eight days.

August 14, 1974: Reinhold Messner and Peter Habeler on-sight the North Face of the Eiger in a record ten hours. News of this ascent inspires Jim Bridwell to respond with an American version of speed climbing: A year later he climbs the Nose In A Day.

June 21, 1975: John Long, Billy Westbay, and Jim Bridwell make the first one-day ascent of the Nose. They take only fifteen hours to cover the route. This is now the canonical speed-climbing goal—Nose In A Day (NIAD).

1975: Reinhold Messner and Peter Habeler make the first alpine-style ascent of an 8,000-meter peak when they climb Hidden Peak, cutting the ascent time for 8,000-meter peaks from months down to days.

June 1978: Galen Rowell and Ned Gillette, a former Olympic cross-country skier, climb Mount McKinley in a single day.

1980: Reinhold Messner solos the North Face of Everest in just three days. It is the first time Everest had ever been soloed, and by far the fastest ascent.

July 14, 1980: Steve Monks (U.K.) on-sight solos the first ascent of the Casual Route on the Diamond, all free, in less than three hours (four years before the normally credited solo by Charlie Fowler).

September 27, 1980: Steve Monks solos the Regular Northwest Face of Half Dome in less than seven hours, using a rope only on pitch 4, the Robbin's Traverse, and above Big Sandy Ledges. The style is quite similar to that used by Dean Potter on the same route eighteen years later, but the ascent isn't publicized and doesn't have an impact on Valley speed climbing.

May 25–28, 1982: Alex MacIntyre, Roger Baxter-Jones, and Doug Scott flash the first ascent of Shishapangma's South Face (8,046 meters). They climb the 2,500-meter face in four days.

June 1982: Christophe Profit free solos the American Direct Route on the Dru in 3:10. He uses a helicopter to approach the route and then is supplied with mixed climbing gear on the summit, but is very open about his style. The route is 3,000 feet high and involves climbing up to 5.11.

Summer 1982: Jim Beyer solos the West Face of El Cap in 23:30. It is the first time El Cap is soloed in a day.

1983: Thomas Budendorfer sets the still-standing solo record of 4.5 hours on the Eiger North Face.

1984: Reinhold Messner and Hans Kammerlander are the first to link up 8,000-meter peaks when they traverse Gasherbrum I and II in four days.

1984: Krzysztof Wielicki makes the first one-day ascent of an 8,000-meter peak when he climbs from base camp to the summit of Broad Peak in seventeen hours. However, this was not a completely solo ascent, and the route had been at least partially prepared.

Summer 1985: Christophe Profit climbs the North Faces of the Eiger (6:45), the Matterhorn (four hours), and the Grandes Jorasses via the Linceul (aka the Shroud; four hours) in a single day. He uses a helicopter to shuttle between the climbs.

July 1985: Ken Evans and Matt Christensen climb Rainier from Paradise to the summit in 3:44. They use running shoes and ski poles the entire way up the glacier route. They do the round-trip in 5:09.

1986: Erhard Loretan and Jean Troillet simul-solo the North Face Direct on Everest in less than two days base camp-to-base camp. They pioneer a bold style of "night nakedness" by climbing without bivouac gear, ropes, harness, protection, etc. They climb mostly at night to stay warm and rest during daylight hours. They glissade the entire face from summit to base in a mere five hours.

June 1986: John Bachar and Peter Croft climb the Nose (10:05) and the Regular Northwest Face of Half Dome (4:05) in a single eighteen-hour day. This is the first linkup of two Grade VI walls in a day.

1988: Marc Batard is the first to climb Everest in a single day (less than twenty-four hours from base camp to summit). The route was previously prepared and it was not a complete solo ascent.

Summer 1988: Steve Schneider and Romain Vogler climb the Nose and the West Face in twenty-three hours. This is the first time El Cap is climbed twice in one day.

May 1989: Steve Schneider becomes the first person to solo the Nose In A Day. He completes the route in 21:22.

Summer 1990: Alain Ghersen enchains the American Direct Route on the Dru with Walker Spur on the Grandes Jorasses and the Great Peuterey Ridge in a single sixty-six-hour marathon.

Summer 1990: Catherine Destivelle solos the Bonatti Pillar on the Dru in five hours.

June 1990: Peter Croft and Dave Schultz climb the Nose and the Salathé in eighteen hours. This is the first and still only time two Grade VI El Cap routes have been climbed in a day.

July 1990: Derek Hersey free solos three routes (Yellow Wall with the Forest Finish, 5.11; Casual Route, 5.10; and Pervertical Sanctuary, 5.10+)—about 25 pitches of climbing—on the Diamond of Longs Peak before 11:00 A.M.

October 2, 1990: Wojciech Kurtyka, Jean Troillet, and Erhard Loretan climb a new route on South Face of Shishapangma in one day. They cut weight even further by carrying no bivouac gear and climbing at night—resting and brewing only during the warmer daylight hours.

October 1990: Steve Gerberding, Scott Stowe, and Rick Lovelace climb the North American Wall in 24:05. While missing the one-day ascent, they prove that hard aid routes can be done in a single push. They also establish the concept of a **push ascent** in contrast to a **one-day ascent.**

Spring 1991: Derek Hersey solos up Scenic Cruise (5.10+), down Leisure Climb (5.9), and then up Journey Home (5.10+). The three routes total more than 30 pitches of climbing. The routes are all in the Black Canyon of the Gunnison in Colorado. Hersey's climbing takes six hours car-to-car.

Summer 1991: Alex Lowe completes the Grand Traverse in 8:15.

Fall 1991: Charlie Fowler solos the 1,800-meter Harlin Direct on the North Face of the Eiger in fourteen hours round-trip.

June 1992: Peter Croft and Hans Florine climb the Nose of El Capitan in 4:22. In the process they take simul-climbing to a new level when one of their "pitches" is 1,000-feet long.

July 1992: Peter Croft and Dave Schultz climb the Rostrum via Excellent Adventure (5.13b, 1:30), the Crucifix (5.12a; 3:30), West Face of El Cap (2:20), and the first three pitches of Astroman (through the first 5.11c pitch) in a day. This is the first time three Grade V routes were linked in a day, free.

June 1993: On his first-ever attempt at soloing, Hans Florine climbs the Nose in 14:10, cutting the solo speed record on the Nose by a third.

Summer 1994: Rolando Garibotti sets the speed records on Lurking Fear (with Jon Rosmergy) and the Shield (with Adam Wainright). This is the first prevalent use of **short-fixing technique** in Yosemite speed climbing.

October 1994: Steve Schneider and Hans Florine climb the Nose, Lurking Fear, and the West Face in 23:01. It is the first and only time three El Cap routes have been done in a day.

Fall 1995: Steve Gerberding, Scott Stowe, and Dave Bengston climb the sustained and difficult Pacific Ocean Wall in 36:24. This route was originally rated A5 and becomes the most difficult route ever climbed in a single push.

Summer 1998: Dean Potter becomes the center of the speed-climbing world with an almost ropeless ascent of the Regular Northwest Face of Half Dome in 4:17. While not pioneering the technique of **ropeless climbing as a means to speed,** Potter takes it into the 5.11 range with big exposure on Half Dome and the Nose.

Summer 1998: Dean Potter sets a host of records with Jose Pereyra, including records on the Salathé Wall (7:33) and Lurking Fear (7:15). They pioneer **use of a Ropeman (microascender) to protect the leader from a second falling off while simul-climbing,** though the technique still hasn't been that widely used.

Summer 1998: Dean Potter climbs Royal Arches (15 pitches, 5.7, A0) in fifty-seven minutes car-to-car, and Snake Dike in three hours car-to-car. This sparks interest in **fast round-trip ascents of moderate routes** that involve running on the approach and the descent.

August 1998: Mike Pennings and Topher Donahue climb Pervertical Sanctuary (5.10+) on the Diamond, solo the North Ridge (5.6) on Spearhead, climb the South Face (5.8) of the Petit Grepon, do the first post-massive-rockfall ascent of the Northcutt-Carter route (5.10) on Hallett Peak's north face, and then climb the Spiral Route (5.4) on Notchtop by headlamp. They start at 3:00 A.M. from the Longs Peak parking lot and finish at the Bear Lake parking lot at 1:30 A.M. the next day.

April 1999: Mike Pennings and Jeff Hollenbaugh link the Touchstone Wall, Space Shot, Monkeyfinger Wall, and Moonlight Buttress in Zion National Park in eighteen hours.

Summer 1999: Dean Potter solos the Casual Route on Longs Peak in a car-to-car time of four hours. This involves a 3,500-vertical-foot approach and then 1,500 feet of up to 5.10 climbing at an elevation of 14,000 feet.

July 26–28, 1999: Dean Potter becomes the first to solo the Nose (in a record time of just under thirteen hours) and the Regular Northwest Face of Half Dome in a day. Potter makes heavy use of leaver biners to protect himself while climbing roped, eliminating the need to descend and clean the gear. With Potter's feat unbeknownst to him, Hans Florine links the same two routes, in reverse order, in 21:40 (setting the solo record of 3:57 on Half Dome in the process).

October 1999: Hans Florine and Jim Herson simul-climb the Regular Northwest Face of Half Dome in 1:53. Herson leads the entire 22-pitch route without ever getting within 100 feet of Florine and they regear only once (by hauling it up on the rope).

May 21, 2000: Babu Chiri Sherpa climbs Everest from Nepal base camp to summit in a record time of 16:56.

Summer 2000: Hans Florine solos Lurking Fear and the West Face of El Cap in a day. It is the first time two El Cap routes have been soloed in a day.

August 26, 2000: Rolando Garibotti solos the Grand Traverse in the Tetons in 6:40, breaking Alex Lowe's mythical time.

September 2000: Teddy Keizer (aka Cave Dog) climbs all fifty-four Colorado Fourteeners in ten days, twenty hours, and twenty-six minutes, breaking the one-year-old previous record by nearly two days.

November 2000: Steve Edwards ascends 400 boulder problems in a day in the Santa Barbara area as part of forty days of birthday challenges leading up to his fortieth birthday.

May 2001: Leo Houlding, after freeing all but the initial bolt ladder, climbs the West Face of the Leaning Tower with Jason "Singer" Smith in 1:59.

June 2001: Steve House and Rolando Garibotti climbed Alaska's Infinite Spur in twenty-five hours. The fastest previous climb was seven days.

November 2001: Dean Potter and Timmy O'Neill climb the Nose in 3:24.

June 2002: Matt Wilder, after making the first free ascent of the South Face of Washington Column, returns with Nick Martino to climb the route in 1:19.

September 2002: Yuji Hirayama and Hans Florine climb the Nose in 2:48. Yuji leads the entire route with one aider and rarely uses it. The team simul-climbs 2,400 feet of the 2,900-foot route, using a Yates Rocker in three sections to protect the leader.

May 2003: Nick Fowler and Yuji Hirayama climb Lurking Fear in 3:04. Yuji leads the entire route, mostly free, frequently unbelayed, as they short-fix furiously.

June 2003: After extensive attempts to free climb the Zodiac, Alex and Thomas Huber speed climb the route three times, the last in 2:38. They return in the fall to free the route.

September 2003: Dean Potter free climbs Half Dome (Regular Northwest Face with variation) and El Cap (via Free Rider) in less than twenty-four hours.

April 2004: Michael Reardon solos 280 routes in nineteen hours at Joshua Tree National Monument. He solos routes up to 5.13 in difficulty.

May 2004: Pempa Dorji Sherpa climbs Mount Everest, using stashed oxygen and fixed camps, from base camp (about 17,000 feet) to the summit (29,035 feet) in just 8:10.

June 2004: Alex and Thomas Huber speed climb the Zodiac in 1:51.

APPENDIX 1
SPEED BETA FOR SPECIFIC ROUTES

When I have finally decided that a result is worth getting, I go ahead on it and make trial after trial until it comes.

—Thomas Edison

Obsessed with the Nose

by Hans Florine

The lifetime goal of many climbers is to climb El Capitan in Yosemite Valley. El Cap is probably the most highly sought after and widely climbed big wall in the world. The reasons are obvious: great weather, no approach, relatively easy descent, perfect rock, variety of lines, etc. Bill and I have a total of sixty-one ascents on the Nose between us.

For aspiring speed climbers the lifetime goal is not just to climb El Cap, but to climb it in a day. While the East Buttress (5.10b, 12 pitches) is clearly on El Cap, it doesn't seem to receive the same distinction as the other routes because it is relatively easy and short. Although other routes like Mr. Midwest (near the West Face) and the Shortest Straw (near the East Buttress) are just as short, they have a level of difficulty that puts them into the "real El Cap route" category.

One of the easiest "real El Cap routes" on the main monolith is also the most famous. It is in the center, it takes the longest straight line, and it is the line of the first ascent—the Nose. "Nose In A Day" (NIAD) is practically a trademarked phrase for speed climbing. It is the feather in every true speed climber's cap. It is the rite of passage, the coup de grâce, the ante-up, and the badge of honor. The Nose follows beautiful cracks, towers, flakes, and corners. It is considered by many to be the greatest pure rock climb in the world. The Nose is relatively free of the scary and physically demanding wide cracks that populate the Salathé, yet has hundreds of feet of fun 5.7 to 5.10 cracks. Heck, the route even goes free at 5.13c/d.

A brief history of fast ascents on the Nose. The first ascent in 1958 took twelve days, and the final push was made by Wayne Mary, James Whitmore, and Warren Harding. In 1960 the first "single push ascent" took six days and was accomplished by Joe Fitschen, Chuck Pratt, Tom Frost, and Royal Robbins. In 1963 a team of three climbed the route in three and a half days. In 1975 the route received its first "one-day" ascent. By the late 1980s numerous teams had done the route in less than a half day, with an Austrian team having done it in nine hours and change. In 1989 Steve Schneider climbed the Nose in less than twenty-four hours solo!

Things got heated in the early 1990s. Steve Schneider and I (H.F.) set the record at 8:05 in 1990. The following week Peter Croft and Dave Shultz did a staggering job of dropping the time to 6:40! In the spring of 1991, Andres Puhvel and I lowered the time to 6:03. The following week Peter and Dave blew everyone's minds with a time of 4:48! In the spring of 1992, Peter Croft and I set the speed record on the Nose at 4:22, which stood until October 2001. On that same day in 1992, Nancy Feagin and Sue McDevitt did the first one-day ascent of the Nose by an all-female team. I set the solo record in 1993 at 14:11; and Dean Potter made it solo in less than thirteen hours in 1999 (then he climbed Half Dome the same day!). As of this printing, Yuji Hirayama and I hold the record at 2:48.

Beta for your NIAD trip. The tricks used to get a sub-six-hour time are extreme and not for most climbers. Not for most speed climbers, in fact. How about the "aspiring speed climber?" Can they also climb the Nose in a day? Yes! A solid 5.10 free climber can climb the Nose in a day. While I don't consider 5.10 crack climbing to be easy, the NIAD is within range of an average weekend warrior who puts in the training and the mileage.

First, do your homework. Work up to a route this big. The Nose is 31 pitches and just shy of 3,000 feet. (If you stretch a 60-meter rope each time, it's 21 pitches, zero simul-climbing.) Try to do a 1,000-foot wall in a day (West Face of Leaning Tower or South Face of Washington Column). Then do a 2,000-foot wall (Northwest Face of Half Dome). Get familiar with the "Big Stone." Do the East Buttress and learn the East Ledges Descent. Do the West Face in a day. Do the Nose in two or three days to learn the route. Climb it again to learn the variations.

Rest for a day or two before the attempt. Make the attempt in June when the days are long and the weather is predictable. You'll go faster with a little extra water weight in the daylight (hot summer days) than you would going lighter (with less water) and climbing in the dark in October. Get to bed early the night before and start climbing the next day at 4:30 A.M. Starting this early maximizes daylight and hopefully reduces night climbing at the end of the day.

The lead line. How long of a lead line? You can use a 50-, 60-, or 70-meter rope. See the detailed topo and read over the information in Chapter 4 about rope selection. I recommend a 60-meter lead line, but there are uses for a 70-meter line if you can conserve gear and stretch it that far—and if you don't mind the extra 10 meters of rope weight.

The rack. The rack for the Nose is largely dependent on the skill and boldness of the leaders. Peter Croft is comfortable running it out 50 feet on 5.10 hand or fist jamming, but the average 5.10 climber will not do this. You might calculate leading with gear every 10 feet when the going is 5.10, every 15 feet at 5.9, and every 20 feet or more when the going is easier. Gear is necessary every 3 to 5 feet when aiding, but the leader can aggressively back clean. These calculations make for a large rack.

You can bring one set of RPs and one set of stoppers, although I've done the whole route placing only one nut. Bring two sets of cams up to 2.5 inches, triples of all could be useful. Selectively, triple up on the 0.5-, 1-, and 2-inch cams, and bring one each of 3-, 3.5-, and 4-inch. Consider two #3s and two #4s if you *really* suck at off-widths. The biggest pieces can ride in the pack most of the time. Bring twelve quickdraws and four to six over-the-shoulder slings with two biners for each (I like to keep these triple looped so they look, ride, and act like quickdraws). Bring two lightweight etriers/aiders and daisy chains (these too can ride in the pack most of the way). The second will need ascenders and Speed Stirrups (slings with a single step, made by Yates), foot loops, or etriers.

Passing other parties. Undoubtedly, you'll have to pass other parties. This route is extremely popular and I've seen as many as nine parties climbing the route at the same time. If the route is overly crowded, you might opt to try another day. Passing is practically mandatory so be prepared for that. See Chapter 6 for passing strategies.

Leading in blocks. The route should be led in blocks. Each climber should clip into the lead line with two locking biners. Not tying directly to the rope allows for quick switching of rope ends. It is best to switch leaders at a good ledge to make the logistics of the changeover easier. Some natural places to switch leaders include Sickle Ledge, Dolt Tower, El Cap Tower, Texas Flake, Boot Flake, Camp IV, Camp V, and Camp VI. Keeping the same leader the whole way is the fastest method.

Pitch by pitch. Approach the first pitch via the 5.7 route "Pine Line" to the left, or up the fifth-class scramble on the right. Pine Line is more direct and easier for hauling (not that you are hauling, are you?) but more technically difficult. Start your watch when you take off from the ledge at the base of the first pitch! (All pitches referred to from here on are as per the topo on pages 134–135.)

You should be able to complete the route in 19 to 32 pitches. If it takes 24 pitches, you need to average sixty minutes a pitch to do the NIAD. Best of luck!

Pitch 1: This pitch is demanding of your free climbing skills. It is one of the few places on the route where you can't easily aid past free moves. Keep an eye out to the right for footholds that help upward progress. All cam sizes work on this pitch.

Pitch 2: This pitch keeps the heat on. You need to pull off a couple free moves with flaring pro placements just prior to grabbing the pendulum point and swinging right to the next crack. Save your 1- to 2-inch cams to leapfrog in the flaring pin scars after the pendulum.

Advanced Tips (AT): You'll need a 70-meter rope to combine the first and second pitches. If you simul-climb either one, remember to have the first "pull" the second up in a counterweight fashion when he lowers for the pendulum.

Pitch 3: This pitch contains more flaring cracks, but bomber placements abound after running it 30 feet off the belay. A bolt ladder consisting of two bolts takes you to fixed gear and another bolt; French freeing this last bolt gets you to 15 feet of 5.9+ climbing and the belay.

AT: You'll need 60.5 meters to combine the second and third pitches.

Pitch 4: This pitch takes you to Sickle Ledge. Climb 15 feet of 5.5–5.6 to a smooth corner; then a single hook move or a 5.10+ stem gains a 1-inch cam placement in a flaring pin scar. After one more flared cam placement, you'll gain fixed gear and bolts, which leads to the first pendulum point. This area has sported all manner of fixed gear and webbing, suffice it to say. Traverse over to the 2-inch, right-facing corner. Pull against this until you can reach up to the fixed swing point here; clip it and swing right for the big ledge that is on the left side of Sickle Ledge. Tall people can stem from the 2-inch, right-facing corner to the huge

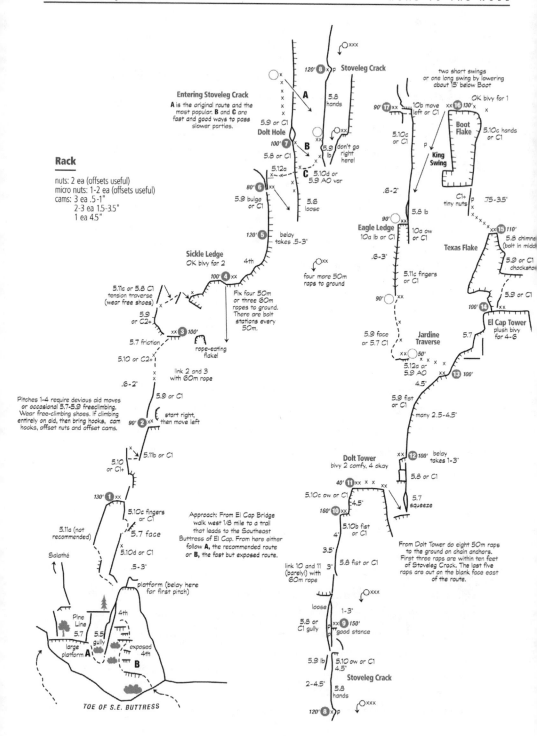

Entering Stoveleg Crack

A is the original route and the most popular. **B** and **C** are fast and good ways to pass slower parties.

120' ⑧ x p **Stoveleg Crack**

5.8 hands

5.9 or C1

Dolt Hole

100' ⑦

5.9 lb don't go right here!

5.8 or C1

5.12a

5.10d or 5.9 AO var

80' ⑥

5.9 bulge or C1

5.6 loose

120' ⑤ belay takes .5-3"

Sickle Ledge
OK bivy for 2

100' ④ xx 4th

Fix four 50m or three 60m ropes to ground. There are bolt stations every 50m.

four more 50m raps to ground

5.11c or 5.8 C1 tension traverse (wear free shoes)

5.9 or C2+

5.7 friction

xx ③ 100'

5.10 or C2+

rope-eating flake!

link 2 and 3 with 60m rope

.6 - 2"

5.9 or C1

90' ② start right, then move left

5.10 or C1+

5.11b or C1

130' ① xx

5.10c fingers or C1

5.11a (not recommended)

5.7 face

Salathé

5.10d or C1

.5 - 3"

platform (belay here for first pitch)

Pine Line

5.7

5.5 gully

4th

large platform **A**

exposed 4th

B

TOE OF S.E. BUTTRESS

Rack

nuts: 2 ea (offsets useful)
micro nuts: 1-2 ea (offsets useful)
cams: 3 ea .5-1"
2-3 ea 1.5-3.5"
1 ea 4.5"

Pitches 1-4 require devious aid moves or occasional 5.7-5.9 freeclimbing. Wear free-climbing shoes. If climbing entirely on aid, then bring hooks, cam hooks, offset nuts and offset cams.

Approach: From El Cap Bridge walk west 1/8 mile to a trail that leads to the Southeast Buttress of El Cap. From here either follow **A**, the recommended route or **B**, the fast but exposed route.

two short swings or one long swing by lowering about 15' below Boot

OK bivy for 1

90' ⑰ xx 10b move left or C1 ⑯ 130'

Boot Flake

5.10c or C1

King Swing

5.10c hands or C1

.6 - 2"

5.8 lb

90'

Eagle Ledge

10a lb or C1

10a ow or C1

C1+ tiny nuts

.75-3.5"

xx ⑮ 110'

5.8 chimne (bolt in middl

Texas Flake

5.9 or C1 chocksto

.6 - 3"

5.11c fingers or C1

5.9 or C1

90'

100' ⑭

El Cap Tower
plush bivy for 4-6

5.9 face or 5.7 C1

Jardine Traverse

5.7

50'

5.12a or 5.9 AO

⑬ 100'

4.5"

5.9 fist or C1

many 2.5-4.5"

Dolt Tower
bivy 2 comfy, 4 okay

xx ⑫ 100' belay takes 1-3"

5.8 or C1

40' ⑪ xx x x xx

5.10c ow or C1

4.5"

5.7 squeeze

160' ⑩ xx

5.10b fist or C1

4'

3.5"

5.8 fist or C1

link 10 and 11 (barely!) with 60m rope

3'

From Dolt Tower do eight 50m raps to the ground on chain anchors. First three raps are within ten feet of Stoveleg Crack. The last five raps are out on the blank face east of the route.

loose

1-3"

5.8 or C1 gully

xx ⑨ 150' good stance

5.9 lb 5.10 ow or C1
4.5"

2-4.5"

5.8 hands

Stoveleg Crack

120' ⑧ x p

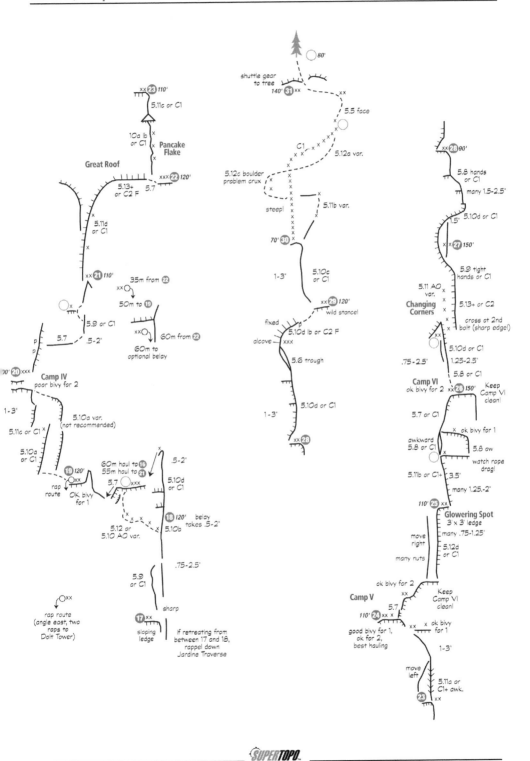

○ 80'

shuttle gear to tree
140' **31** xx

23 110'
5.11c or C1

10a lb or C1

Pancake Flake

Great Roof

xxx **22** 120'
5.13+ or C2 F   5.7

5.11d or C1

21 110'

35m from **22**

50m to **19**

5.5 face

C1   5.12a var.

5.12c boulder problem crux

steep!   5.11b var.

70' **30**

1-3"   5.10c or C1

25 120'   wild stance!

5.10d lb or C2 F

5.6 trough

5.10d or C1

1-3"

28

5.7   .5-2"

60m from **22**

60m to optional belay

20 100' xxx

Camp IV
poor bivy for 2

1-3"

5.10a var. (not recommended)

5.11c or C1

5.10a or C1

19 120'
rap route

OK bivy for 1

60m haul to **16**
55m haul to **21**

5.7

.5-2"

5.10d or C1

18 120'   belay takes .5-2"
5.12 or 5.10 AO var.   5.10b

.75-2.5"

5.9 or C1

○ xx

rap route
(angle east, two raps to Dolt Tower)

17 xx
sloping ledge

sharp

if retreating from between 17 and 18, rappel down Jardine Traverse

26 90'
5.8 hands or C1
many 1.5-2.5"

1.5"   5.10d or C1

27 150'

5.9 tight hands or C1

5.11 AO var.

Changing Corners

5.13+ or C2
cross at 2nd bolt (sharp edge!)

5.10d or C1

.75-2.5"   1.25-2.5"

5.8 or C1

Camp VI
ok bivy for 2   **26** 150'   Keep Camp VI clean!

5.7 or C1

ok bivy for 1

awkward 5.8 or C1   5.8 ow
watch rope drag!

5.11b or C1+   3.5"
many 1.25.-2"

110' **25** xx

Glowering Spot
3'x 3' ledge
many .75-1.25"

move right

5.12d or C1

many nuts

ok bivy for 2

Keep Camp VI clean!

Camp V   5.7

110' **24** xx x

good bivy for 1,
ok for 2,
best hauling

ok bivy for 1

1-3"

move left

5.11a or C1+ awk.

23 xx

flake that marks the left side of Sickle. If you are trailing a rope, watch the rope-eating flake on the far left side of Sickle, down about 50 feet.

Sickle Ledge is considered to be one-tenth of the way up the route. Fractional marks are given so you can check your time and see how you're doing. These fractions are *not* length in distance climbed but the time consumed at that point for a one-day ascent. For example, if it takes you and your partner three hours to get to Sickle, your team will likely take thirty hours to complete the route. If you only have supplies for a fourteen-hour ascent, you should consider backing off.

Pitch 5: Scramble up fourth class and 5.4 to the upper right side of Sickle Ledge.

Pitch 6: This pitch is 5.5 up to a short steep 5.9+ crack that takes you out around the corner onto the face where a bolted belay awaits you.

AT: From the big chain anchors on Sickle, it is 62 meters to the end of the sixth pitch, just out of the top of Sickle. With a tiny bit of simul-climbing, you can combine the fifth pitch (fourth class) with the sixth pitch (5.9). The second is on easy fourth-class terrain, while the leader is going up the 5.6 and 5.9.

Pitch 7: Lower off the anchor about 40 or more feet and swing over to the left-facing corner that leads up to Dolt Hole. Climb as high as you feel comfortable before placing gear to make it easier on the follower when they lower over. Put in the belay about 20 feet down from Dolt Hole.

(*NOTE*: Get out the big gear for pitches 8–14.)

Pitch 8 (B variation per topo): Lower down to tension traverse right along the bolted 5.10d variation. You are now in the Stovelegs. Do *not* go one more crack to the right! Again, climb as high as you feel comfortable before putting in protection. This 0.75- to 1.5-inch lieback crack leads into the most beautiful 2-inch hand jamming section of the route. After 80 feet of 5.8 hand jamming, you'll reach a 3-inch crack and then a fixed bong and a ⅜-inch bolt for a belay. These are at a turn in the crack before the crack gets small again.

AT (pitch 5–8): Simul-climb pitches 5 and 6 as suggested earlier. When the leader lowers off the sixth anchor to do the tension traverse, have him "pull" the second up in a counterweight fashion. Keep simul-climbing while the leader goes up the dihedral to Dolt Hole. If the second needs a belay for the final 15 feet to the sixth belay, then the leader can slam in a couple of pieces and belay the second on that section before continuing.

About 20 feet below Dolt Hole, you'll find a ¼-inch bolt, often with tat on it, on the face 5 feet right of the crack. Clip this bolt and do another tension traverse to the very bottom of the Stovelegs. Continue up the Stoveleg crack until you run out of rope. With a 60-meter rope, you'll be able to reach the eighth belay while the second is still at the sixth anchor. Remember, after each pendulum wait as long as possible to put in your first piece or the rope drag will kill you, and the follower will have a harder time lowering out. With this method the rope is stretched tight; the second will need a lower-out line. Either bring a 110-foot length of ⅞-millimeter rope or a full 60-meter length to use in case retreat is needed.

You can combine pitch 7 and 8 without simul-climbing. However, it's possible to lower off the sixth anchor while belaying the climber in the Stovelegs and continue simul-climbing until the leader runs out of gear. Peter and I simul-climbed all the way to the top of pitch 16 from the top of pitch 4!

(NOTE: This is a good area to pass another party. Because there are three ways to move from the Dolt Hole crack system to the Stovelegs, it is possible to go around a slower party here without impeding their climbing.)

Pitch 9–11: These three pitches up to Dolt Tower can be combined into two pitches with a 60-meter rope. Just run out the rope and construct a belay from gear or fixed pieces wherever you end up. The last 130 feet to the top of Dolt Tower is a great stretch to leapfrog #3 and #4 cams. You've got to keep them with you until the end unless you bring two of each. On top of Dolt Tower, you are one-quarter of the way up the route. If you planned on a fourteen-hour ascent and it took you eight hours to get here, you had better consider backing off. (Convenient 50-meter rap stations lead to the ground from here.)

Pitch 12: The leader lowers off the right side of Dolt Tower and then goes up the 5.9 crack. After wrestling in a wide flaring chimney crack, you'll reach great bear-hugging cracks that are side by side. Transfer to the right one as you near the anchor, which is a fixed pin and two nice

⅜-inch bolts. The leader should back-clean low on this pitch to make the swing or lower out easier for the follower. This creates less rope drag and makes it easier to combine the next pitch. The second either lowers out on a fixed line (one is usually there) or the lower-out line, or can easily downclimb and cross to the crack.

Pitch 13: This is a well-protected crack to a 3- to 4-inch corner crack up to a large ledge. The pitch ends with a bolted belay at the base of the Jardine Traverse.

AT: You'll need 56 meters to combine pitches 12 and 13. Once at the top of the thirteenth pitch, you can put away the big gear until pitch 26, but keep out one 3.5-inch cam.

(*NOTE*: Most parties take a long time to deal with pitches 14–19. Consider taking the Jardine variation to the left at the top of pitch 13. It is faster than the original route.)

Pitch 14: Combine the fourteenth pitch up to El Cap Tower and the Texas Flake pitch (pitch 15) with easy simul-climbing, or just go to El Cap Tower. Belay from El Cap Tower or from the front of Texas Flake.

Pitch 15: Get behind the Texas Flake by going around the right/east side. Climb the Texas Flake by facing out on the west side of the flake (west side of the route). You can reach around and grab the front of the flake once you get up high enough. The Texas Flake pitch features a bolt that protects the chimney somewhat, but unfortunately the bolt is on the east side. It's best not to clip the bolt so you can flip the rope to the outside of the flake allowing the follower the luxury of not having to jug inside the flake. The top of this flake is one-third of the way up the route.

Pitch 16: This is the Boot Flake, an easy bolt ladder to a thin and slowly widening crack—easy to French free.

AT: You can combine pitch 16 with the Texas Flake pitch. It is less than 60 meters from the base of the Texas Flake to the top of the Boot. Or, do it with some simul-climbing, which isn't as radical as it seems. The Texas Flake pitch requires (or even allows for) little gear. This leaves you plenty for the next pitch, which is half bolt ladder and half thin hand crack. While the leader is climbing the 5.10c hands or the bolt ladder, the second is climbing relatively easy ground up to the Texas Flake and doing the chimney behind.

Pitch 17: Do the King Swing by lowering down until you're 15 feet below the bottom of Boot Flake. This is even with the last bolt of the bolt ladder leading to Boot Flake. Run to the right first and take one long swing into the corner and crack, which leads into the gray bands. The leader must now back-clean all the gear while climbing up to the seventeenth belay anchor and beyond. The safest way to do this is for the leader to lead as high as is comfortable without gear, place gear normally until the rope drag gets bad, and then place a couple of bomber pieces and lower down to clean the bottom pieces. Lather, rinse, and repeat. The leader continues this strategy up to the seventeenth belay anchor.

Pitch 18: Lead up to the right side of the ledge that the nineteenth belay anchor is on.

AT: You can keep stretching the lead after the King Swing to the top of the nineteenth pitch or to the right side of the ledge that the 19th belay anchor is on. The second follows this pitch by lowering out on a lower line or with the remaining rope end. The leader must stop at (or between) the belay for pitches 17 and 18 if you have no lower-out line because the follower will need all the extra rope for the lower out. After the King Swing, I try to wait until I am above the seventeenth belay before I leave my first piece of protection. This makes the lower out a ton easier for the follower.

AT (pitches 15–17): Here's beta for the "super advanced." When the leader lowers off the top of the Boot Flake, and while the second is simul-climbing or belaying from the top of the Texas Flake, have the leader clean all pieces on the Boot down to the highest bolt on the bolt ladder. The follower can be "getting a counterweight" here, or just sit on top of the Texas Flake. The leader then does the King Swing over to Eagle Ledge and clips in to the fixed rope. The follower then jugs or climbs up to the last bolt on the ladder and also pendulums over. When the leader starts to climb again, the belayer is pulling the rope from the anchors on top of the Boot Flake.

Pitch 19: For this pitch, get up to the ledge via the bolted face climbing or go up cracks and lower down onto the ledge. Traverse left on fourth class terrain, execute one 5.7 downclimb move, and scamper over to a bolted belay.

Pitches 20-21: Climb up 5.11c or A0 to Camp IV, then continue on 100 feet of 5.9 up and over to the base of the Great Roof pitch. These two pitches can be combined into one. It is less than 60 meters from the nineteenth belay anchor to the twenty-first. When the follower goes past Camp IV, you're at the halfway point. You want to be here in well under twelve hours for the NIAD.

AT: Have the second cruise across the anchor nineteen ledge while the leader is going up pitch 20. Consider short-fixing to Camp IV and self-belay leading up pitch 21 while the follower is jugging.

Pitch 22: Although pitch 22 is only 110 feet, it takes a bunch of gear and time. Leapfrog ⅜-, ½-, and ¾-inch cams, and clip the fixed pins and nuts.

Pitch 23: This pitch is spectacular and has possibly the best lieback crack in the world. It would be a shame not to free this 70 feet of glory—clipping fixed pieces and a few 1-inch cam placements gets you through it to a nice triangle ledge. Here, a very thin section leads up; use your smallest cams and small nuts until the crack widens to ¾- and 1-inch. About 20 feet of 5.7 ledge-mantling leads to bolted anchors.

AT: Upon reaching the twenty-second belay anchor, pull up all the slack, fix the rope, and self-belay lead the Pancake Flake while the follower is jugging/cleaning pitch 22. From the triangle ledge at the top of the Pancake Flake, you can reach Camp V in one rope length.

Pitch 24: On this pitch, keep an eye out for a place where you can get out of the flaring corner and reach into the nice 1-inch crack on the left. Things move faster out of the flare. End pitch 24 on any of the Camp V ledges because pitch 25 is pretty short.

Pitch 25: This is a tough aid or free lead (thin nut placements). Keep an eye out for a place where you can get into the crack on your right in the corner. Leapfrogging cams in this crack goes faster than tinkering in the seam.

Pitch 26: Be ready to leapfrog your 1-inch, then 2-inch, and finally 3- and 4-inch cams on this pitch. If you're up for it, this pitch is a wonderful, albeit hard, 5.11 hand crack to free climb. Stay on the left side of all the blocky ledges up to Camp VI.

AT: Haul up some line when you reach the Glowering Spot and fix the rope. Lead on self-belay up pitch 26 while the follower is cleaning pitch 25.

Pitch 27: Eighty feet off Camp VI you can go into the dihedral on the right down low or higher after going up the 5.11 sport bolts on the left. If you're six feet or taller, the sport bolts can be French freed at 5.11a. It's much faster than aiding the dihedral.

AT: If you led to the very end of a 60-meter rope every time from Camp VI up (regardless of where you belayed), you'd be off in 3 pitches.

Pitch 28: This is a strenuous 5.10+ hand crack. Leapfrog with 1- and 2-inch pieces if not freeing the pitch.

Pitch 29: This pitch eats up pieces from 0.75 to 1.5 inches.

Pitch 30: A tricky face move gets you into the crack; this pitch is fun 5.10 liebacking and very short.

Pitch 31: This pitch takes a bunch of draws; definitely back-clean every other one. If you skip more than that, you risk making it hard for the second to clean. The easy hauling anchor is a nice airy spot—definitely worth a pause to gape down the route.

AT: Pitch 30 and 31 are short enough to combine, but rope drag can easily foil that plan. Consider short-fixing the lead rope 25 feet above where it turns the lip, and self-belay from there to the top while your partner is jugging the steep bolted section. From the bolts at the thirty-first belay, you can walk up slabs to a tree and celebrate in the shade. (Unless you topped out in the dark!) These bolts are where a NIAD time is considered stopped (as per every reported ascent I know of).

Beta on the Maiden

by Bill Wright

The Maiden is one of the fabled Flatirons that dot the mountain slope above Boulder, Colorado. While most Flatirons possess a low-angle east slab, the Maiden is sheer on all sides and is the most striking summit in the Boulder area. The famed rappel from the summit drops a hundred feet down the massively overhung west face to the Crow's Nest, which is perched on a thin fin of rock with sheer drops on both sides.

Climbs ranging in difficulty from 5.6 to 5.13 lead to the summit, with the most traveled route being the classic and unusual North Face route (5.6). This route is listed as one of local guidebook author Gerry Roach's Top Ten. The route is devious, deciphering a path to the summit that

The Maiden

consists mostly of downclimbing and traversing. I particularly like climbing the Maiden because of the approach, which is somewhat long and arduous compared to most Boulder climbs. By combining a brisk approach with an efficient climb, this route can be done in less than two hours, car-to-car. (Hey, that's a long lunch or a good adventure for before or after work!) I'll describe here a fast strategy for simul-climbing or rope soloing this route.

Since the approach is long, going as light as possible is key. The route is only 5.6, so consider climbing in a sticky rubber approach shoe—that way you don't have to carry shoes. Bring a light, alpine harness, a locking carabiner, and a rappel device. I like to wear a small CamelBak like the

H.A.W.G. for these adventures and bring along about a liter of water. The rappels require a single 60-meter rope. Both rappels are very close to one hundred feet, so be very careful to get the rope exactly even. I use a 7.8 mm rope for this climb because it is so light. How much gear you bring depends upon whether you are soloing, rope soloing, or simul-climbing. I'll specify the placements below and you can decide, but the total rack consists of at most two cams and five slings. That's it. This is light enough so that you can run the trail in and out, if desired.

The best trailhead to use is the South Mesa Trailhead. I prefer to follow the Mesa Trail to the Big Bluestem Trail and then head up the Big Bluestem to where it reconnects with the Mesa Trail. Go south to a bridge trail that connects to Shadow Canyon. This point can be reached by staying on the Mesa Trail, but it involves a bit more climbing. Head up the bridge trail for a minute or two before breaking off to the right (west) on a faint climber's trail. This leads to an old road grade and from there the trail is very clear as it heads directly west and very steeply up the slope to the looming Maiden. The approach is about 2.5 miles and gains nearly two thousand feet.

The North Face route starts directly west of the Maiden. You start by climbing a short, 25-foot wall, which is a fin of the Maiden. Once atop this wall, the Maiden rears up in front of you like a giant stone cobra. You are looking directly at the 5.11 West Overhang route. Climb down the fin to the Crow's Nest, which is at the base of the overhang. The climbing here is very easy (fourth class), but gets quite exposed as you near the Crow's Nest because the fin narrows to about a foot in width; you'll have to drop off the north side and use the fin as a hand rail.

Solo the first part of the climb to the Crow's Nest. If the exposure is too great, you can place an Alien (yellow) or two along the final section. Once at the Crow's Nest, climb up the West Overhang route for just ten feet to a good crack. Place a one-inch cam here with a long sling. This will protect the crux moves. If you are rope soloing, you'll be able to retrieve this piece after the first rappel. If you are rope-soloing, tie both ends of the rope to your harness to form a big loop. You can use a Grigri or knots to adjust the size of this loop. Clip your loop to this piece above the Crow's Nest.

Climb down the ramp on the north side until you are just about the same height as the tree on the ledge farther east. There is a fixed piton here that you can clip with a long sling, but it isn't necessary due to the piece you placed above the Crow's Nest. Hand traverse left to easy ground. If rope soloing, untie one end of your loop and pull it through the piece at the Crow's Nest.

Put a sling around the tree here and clip your rope (or your loop) into this piece. If rope soloing, this will be a leaver piece, as it will not be retrieved. Is the climb worth purposely leaving behind a sling and biner? It depends. I rope soloed this route in January of 2004 and when I returned in April, the leaver biner and sling were still there. Since I was now climbing with a partner, I was able to retrieve my gear.

From the tree, climb up and left across the face, past a couple of fixed pitons. Clip the pins as desired, but if you are rope soloing, these will likely be leaver biners. This variation is known as the Walton Traverse and it is the best and fastest route on the North Face. It is possible to go low here and around the corner, but it is much more difficult to pull your rope across if you do this. Getting your rope stuck here puts you in a very stressful position. If you are rope soloing your only option is to down-climb to fix the problem.

Once you reach the ledge at the end of the Walton Traverse, pull your rope across, coil it and put it on your back. From here on up the difficulties are about fourth class. Scoot up a chimney and then work your way directly onto the East Ridge. Don't continue straight to the summit, but contour out to the east. Once on the ridge the going is very easy, and in a minute or two you'll be on the summit.

Two single-rope rappels with your 60-meter rope will get you back to the ground on the south side of the Maiden. After the first rappel to the Crow's Nest, make sure you go retrieve the piece you placed just above here on the ascent. Then coil the rope and reverse your approach back to the car.

Here are some times to beat. Bill Briggs did an unroped solo ascent of the Maiden from the trailhead in one hour and twenty-three minutes. Buzz Burrell and I completed the route as a two-man roped team in one hour and thirty-six minutes. I did a roped solo of the route from the trailhead in one hour and fifty-eight minutes.

APPENDIX 2
SPEED RECORDS

It's a Record!

It seems that anywhere there is a landmark mountain there is a speed record for the ascent, no matter the difficulty of the route, be it hiking terrain or technical rock climbing. The Canadians track perhaps the most hilarious speed record. The beautiful, multiturreted Castle Mountain has a small alpine hut 1,500 feet below the summit on the airy plateau. It is 3,000 vertical feet above the trailhead. The reported round-trip record for descending from the hut, driving to the liquor store, and returning is around two hours and forty minutes.

The Web site for Yosemite speed climbing records is www.Speedclimb .com, and links to other areas are on this site as well. Colorado speed records have not been as meticulously recorded or as avidly pursued as Yosemite big wall records. Nevertheless, some times have been recorded in guidebooks and through word of mouth. The site www.speedclimb-ing.org is an attempt to keep a more formal record of worldwide speed climbs. E-mail in your ascents!

Below is a selected collection of speed climbs from around the world. There is no way this can be complete or even up to date, as these things change frequently, but it might provide a bit of motivation. For a more complete and up-to-date list, see the sites mentioned above and the links on those sites.

NOTE: The time format is almost always hours:minutes, but for some of the shorter routes the format is hours:minutes:seconds.

Speed Records

El Capitan
West Face:
1:56:16   Timmy O'Neill and Hans Florine; November 1999

5:56	Lisa Coleman-Puhvel and Hans Florine; October 1998 (fastest female/male ascent)
8:16	Hans Florine—solo; June 2000 (soloed two El Cap routes in a day)

Lurking Fear:

3:04:54	Yuji Hirayama and Nick Fowler; May 2003
9:20	Hans Florine—solo; June 2000 (soloed two El Cap routes in a day)

The Salathé:

6:32	Jim Herson and Chandlee Harrell; July 1999 (free variation on pitches 24 and 32)
27:20	Sue McDevitt and Nancy Feagin; June 1998 (all female)
23:20	Steve Schneider—solo; June 1992
13:00	Yuji Hirayama; May 2002 (fastest free ascent)

The Shield:

10:58	Cedar Wright and Chris McNamara; August 1999

Muir:

19:57	Niles and Brian McCray; June 2001

Triple Direct:

8:20	Adam Wainwright and Rolo Garibotti; mid-1990s

The Nose:

2:48:55	Yuji Hirayama and Hans Florine; September 2002
12:15	Heidi Wertz and Vera Shulte-Pelcum; June 2004 (all female ascent)
12:59	Dean Potter—solo; July 1999 (start of El Cap and Half Dome in a day)
23:46	Lynn Hill; 1994 (fastest free ascent)

North American Wall:

9:36	Tim O'Neill and Miles Smart; September 1999

Tangerine Trip:

10:24	Cedar Wright and Ammon McNeely; July 2002

Zodiac:

1:51	Alex and Thomas Huber; June 2004

East Buttress:

00:43	Hans Florine—solo; July 2000 (2:09 car-to-car)
2:20	Jason "Singer" Smith and Miles Smart; 1999 (car-to-car)

Half Dome

Tis-sa-ack:

12:00   Sean Kriletich and Jake Whitaker; 2000

Direct Northwest Face:

8:20   Dean Potter and Jose Pereyra; 1998

11:25   Miles Smart—solo; September 1999

Regular Northwest Route:

1:53:25   Jim Herson and Hans Florine; October 1999

5:25   Heidi Wertz and Vera Shulte-Pelcum; June 2004 (all female ascent)

3:58   Hans Florine—solo; July 1999 (start of Half Dome and El Cap in a day)

Snake Dike:

3:00   Dean Potter; 1998 (car-to-car)

Washington Column

South Face:

1:19   Matt Wilder and Nick Martino; June 2002

The Prow:

3:01   Jason "Singer" Smith and Cedar Wright; June 2001

6:31   Willie Benegas—solo; October 1999

Royal Arches

Royal Arch Route:

0:52:26   Cedar Wright—solo; May 2000 (car-to-car)

Joshua Tree National Monument

280 Routes In A Day:

19:00   Michael Reardon—solo; April 2004

Colorado

Casual Route on the Diamond:

4:00   Dean Potter—solo; 1999 (car-to-car)

Spearhead's North Ridge:

3:22   Kelly Cordes—solo; July 2003 (car-to-car)

Bastille Crack:

0:5:33   Mic Fairchild—solo; July 1998

0:12:46   Bill Wright and Hans Florine; April 2002

Yellow Spur:

    0:12:40   Mic Fairchild—solo; June 1998

    0:58:10   Josh Wharton and Kevin Cochran (footbridge-to-footbridge)

Naked Edge:

    1:00:05   Josh Wharton and Phil Gruber; August 2003 (ground to top of route)

Third Flatiron:

    0:36:27   Bill Briggs—solo; July 1989 (car-to-car)

Zion

Moonlight Buttress:

    1:57   Ammon McNeely and "Fly'n Brian" McCray; February 2003

Spaceshot:

    1:36   Ammon McNeely and "Fly'n Brian" McCray; October 2003

Touchstone Wall:

    1:50   Doug Heinrich and Seth Shaw; 1992

Prodigal Son:

    2:36   Ammon McNeely and "Fly'n Brian" McCray; February 2003

Red Rocks, Nevada

Epinephrine:

    1:15   Josh Swartz—solo; 2002

Levitation 20/Cloud Tower/Epinephrine linkup:

    20:07   Ivo Ninov and Renan Ozturk; 2004 (car-to-car)

Alaska

Mount McKinley:

    23:56   Chad Kellogg—solo; 2003 (landing strip-to-landing strip)

New Hampshire

Moby Grape:

    1:03   Tim Kemple—solo; 2002

The Gunks, New York

50 Routes:

    13:30   Peter Darmi—solo; September 2004

46 Routes:

    13:30   Eric Weigeshoff and Peter Darmi; September 2004

Wyoming

Grand Traverse:

6:40   Rolando Garibotti—solo; 2000

Grand Teton:

1:55   Creighton King—solo; 1983

3:06   Bryce Thatcher—solo; 1983 (car-to-car)

Europe

Mount Elbrus:

1:40   Anatoli Boukreev; 1990

Eiger North Face:

4:50   Thomas Bubendorfer; 1983

Matterhorn:

3:14   Bruno Brunod; 1995 (round-trip from Cervinia)

Mont Blanc:

5:15   Pierre Gignoux and Stéphane Brosse; 2003 (round-trip from Chamonix)

South America

Aconcagua:

3:40   Jean Pellissier, Bruno Brunod, Fabio Meraldi; February 2000

Cerro Torre:

8:30   Dean Potter—solo; 2002 (via Compressor Route)

Fitzroy:

6:30   Dean Potter—solo; 2002 (via Super Couloir)

Africa

Kilimanjaro:

12:45   John Winsor and Kevin Cooney; 1994

Asia

Mount Everest:

8:10   Pempa Dorji Sherpa; May 2004

Dhaulagiri:

17:15   Anatoli Boukreev; October 1995

Shishapangma:

12:00   Fabio Meraldi

GLOSSARY

Many climbing terms are used in this book but are not included in this glossary. The terms that appear below are unique to, or prevalent in, speed climbing.

batmanning: when a climber goes up the rope hand over hand like Batman and Robin do on the side of a building.

bivy: short for the French word "bivouac," which means to sleep without shelter.

block: a collection of consecutive pitches on a long climb.

caterpillar technique: a method usually used by a three-person team to climb a route. One person jugs a free line, one of the top two leads, and the third is cleaning the pitch below. This term gets confused with short-fixing by some (including Hans). See short-fixing.

etrier: used instead of an aid ladder, the steps alternate on each side of a center piece of webbing.

flash: free climbing a route on your first attempt with the help of either some specific beta or by watching someone else first.

follower: see second.

free solo: usually means an unroped free solo, but technically it could mean a roped (not aided) solo ascent.

French free climbing: Climbing by pulling, pushing, or standing on pieces of gear (cams, bolts, etc.) as if they were natural holds, but not by standing in slings or aiders. Used for short, hard sections.

Grigri: a mechanical belay/rappel device that allows for hands-free belaying; manufacturer recommends that you keep a hand on the brake end of the rope.

in a day: doing an ascent "in a day" means that it took less than twenty-four hours; can be spread over two calendar days, as in Lynn Hill's "in a day" free ascent of the Nose.

leader: the first climber to ascend the pitch and place the protection.

leading in blocks: a way to climb that is frequently faster than swapping leads; the leader stays out in front for a set of pitches instead of switching every pitch.

leaver biner: a carabiner that is used and left behind; used while roped soloing so that the climber doesn't need to descend to retrieve them; also used for lowering out on a traverse.

NIAD: Nose In A Day.

no bivys: Hans's mantra and the essence of this book. Climbing without a bivouac.

on-sight: climbing a route on your first attempt with no previous knowledge of the route, save the grade; more often applied to free climbing.

piece: any protection device such as nuts, camming units, pitons (aka pins), etc.

pinkpoint: free climbing a route that you've attempted before, using pre-placed gear; most sport climbers now call this a redpoint.

portaledge: portable cot-like structure that is hauled up a route, assembled, and attached to the rock in order to have a comfortable place to sleep.

push ascent: an ascent that is done without a bivy but takes longer than a normal climbing day, usually more than twenty-four hours.

redpoint: free climbing a route that you've attempted before; all gear must be placed on lead except for fixed gear such as bolts; climbers have equated this term to pinkpointing.

Reverso: a Petzl belay device used for belaying a leader or follower. Great for multitasking.

roped solo: soloing using a rope for protection.

second: also called follower; climber who follows the pitch and cleans gear the leader has placed; the second and the leader frequently switch roles during a long climb.

short-fixing: a technique that allows the leader to get a jump on the next pitch by tying off the rope for the follower and continuing with a self-belay. See also caterpillar technique.

Silent Partner: a mechanical belay device used for roped solo climbing.

simul-climbing: roped climbing where both the leader and the other climber(s) on the rope are moving at the same time.

simul-seconding: a technique where the leader leads normally, sets up a belay, and belays two following climbers either on separate ropes or on the same rope; the followers are climbing at the same time.

simul-seconding on a single rope: same as simul-seconding except that both climbers are tied into the same rope; usually one climber is on the end of the rope and the other is tied in about 20 or 30 feet from the end.

simul-soloing: climbing unroped but with a partner; a technique frequently used in alpine climbing when ascending moderate couloirs or covering fourth-class terrain; a common way to climb many of the classic Flatiron slab routes above Boulder, Colorado.

soloing: climbing alone, whether free or aid, roped or unroped; frequently used in place of the more descriptive "unroped free solo."

Soloist: a mechanical belay device used for roped solo climbing.

third classing: an unroped free solo; comes from the International Mountaineering and Climbing Federation (UIAA) climbing classification that states a third-class climb is a scramble that does not involve a rope; so when someone says he "third classed" a 5.10 route (which is Class 5), it means that he climbed it as if it was third class (i.e., he didn't use a rope).

unroped solo: once meant unequivocally an unroped free solo, but with Russ Mitrovich's unroped aid solo of the Zodiac, it can only be taken to mean "climbing without a rope."

unroped free solo: climbing without a rope and freeing all the moves.

unroped French free solo: soloing without a rope and pulling on gear and/or aiding.

unroped aid solo: climbing a route using aid alone and without the use of a rope; *see* **unroped solo** and insane.

Wall Hauler: a combination pulley/camming device that makes hauling a bag much easier; indispensable when trying to haul the bag and belay the second at the same time; a Grigri comes in handy as the belay device in this situation.

FURTHER READING
AND REFERENCES

Books

Anker, Daniel, ed. *Eiger: the Vertical Arena*. Seattle, Washington: The Mountaineers, 2000.

Arce, Gary. *Defying Gravity—High Adventure on Yosemite's Walls*. Berkeley, California: Wilderness Press, 1996.

Ardito, Stephano. *Mont Blanc*. Seattle, Washington: The Mountaineers, 1997.

Bridwell, Jim. *Climbing Adventures*. Merrillville, Indiana: ICS Books, 1992.

Brookfield, John. *Mastery of Hand Strength*. Ironmaid Enterprises, 1995.

Collister, Rob. *Lightweight Expeditions*. Ramsbury, Marlborough, England: The Crowood Press, 1989.

Duane, Dan. *El Capitan*. San Francisco, California: Chronicle Books, 2000.

Fanshawe, Andy, and Stephen Venables. *Himalaya Alpine-Style*. Seattle, Washington: The Mountaineers, 1995.

Frison-Roche, Roger, and Sylvain Jouty. *A History of Mountain Climbing*. New York, New York: Flammarion, 1996.

Godfrey, Robert, and Dudley Chelton. *Climb!* Boulder, Colorado: American Alpine Club, 1977.

Hepp, Tilmann, and Wolfgang Gullich. *A Life in the Vertical*. Stuttgart, Germany: Boulder Ed., 1994.

Jones, Chris. *Climbing in North America*. Berkeley, California: University of California Press, 1976.

Kroese, Mark. *Fifty Favorite Climbs of North America*. Seattle, Washington: The Mountaineers, 2002.

Lee, Chip. *On Edge: The Life & Climbs of Henry Barber*. Boston, Massachusetts: Appalachian Mountain Club, 1982.

Long, John. *The High Lonesome*. Helena, Montana: Falcon Publishing, 1999.

_____. *Rock Jocks, Wall Rats and Hangdogs*. New York, New York: Fireside, 1994.

Long, John, and Craig Luebben. *Advanced Rock Climbing*. Conifer, Colorado: Chockstone Press, 1997.

Messner, Reinhold. *The Big Walls*. New York, New York: Oxford University Press, 1978.

Meyers, George. *Yosemite Climber*. Modesto, California: Diadem Books/Robbins Mountain Letters, 1979.

Meyers, George, and Don Reid. *Yosemite Climbs*. Denver, Colorado: Chockstone Press, 1987. (The history section of this edition of the Yosemite guidebook [by Meyers] is the best overall reference for free climbing history. Later editions by Reid [1995, 1999] do not include this section.)

Rand, Ayn. *Atlas Shrugged*. New York, New York: Random House Inc., 1957.

Roper, Steve. *Camp 4*. Seattle, Washington: The Mountaineers, 1994.

_____. *Climber's Guide to Yosemite*. San Francisco, California: Sierra Club, 1971.

Roper, Steve, and Allen Steck. *Fifty Classic Climbs of North America*. San Francisco, California: Sierra Club, 1979.

Roth, Arthur. *Eiger: Wall of Death*. London, England: Victor Gollancz Ltd., 1982.

Rowell, Galen. *High and Wild: Essays and Photographs on Wilderness Adventure*. San Francisco, California: Lexikos, 1983.

_____. *The Vertical World of Yosemite*. Berkeley, California: Wilderness Press, 1974.

Salkeld, Audrey. *World Mountaineering*. London, England: Octopus Publishing Group Ltd., 1998.

Scott, Chic. *Pushing the Limits*. Calgary, Alberta, Canada: Rocky Mountain Books, 2000.

Scott, Doug. *Big Wall Climbing*. London, England: Oxford University Press, 1974.

Twight, Mark F., and James Martin. *Extreme Alpinism*. Seattle, Washington: The Mountaineers, 1999.

Unsworth, Walt. *Savage Snows: The Story of Mont Blanc*. London, England: Hodder and Stoughton Limited, 1986.

Whymper, Edward. *Scrambles Amongst the Alps*. Berkeley, California: Ten Speed Press, 1981. (Originally published in 1871.)

Articles

Achey, Jeff. "Balancing Act." *Climbing* magazine 189 (1999): 74–81, 142–43.

Bridwell, Jim. "Brave New World." *Mountain* 31 (1973).

Duane, Dan. "Up on the Big Stone." *Outside Magazine* (October 2000): 80–88.

Gore, Peter. "The Unbeatable Body." *National Geographic* (September 2000): 32.

O'Neill, Timothy. "Yosemite Speed, Patagonia Summits." *American Alpine Journal* (2000): 66–74.

Pagel, Dave. "Great Innovations." *Climbing* magazine 192, (2000): 120–131.

Raleigh, Duane. "Get on the Fast Track." *Climbing* magazine 148 (November 1994): 146–151.

Raleigh, Duane, and Dave Anderson. "Tech Tip: Aid Climbing." *Climbing* magazine 189 (November 1999): 132.

Schneider, Steve. "Seize the Day." *Climbing* magazine 153 (June 1995): 90–99

Sharp, Alec. "Who's Your Friend?" *Mountain* 69 (September/October 1979.)

Thesenga, Jonathan. "The A Team." *Climbing* magazine 192 (March 2000): 104–112.

Web Sites

www.Speedclimb.com (Hans Florine's site about Yosemite Valley speed climbing records.)

www.speedclimbing.org (Bill Wright's site on Colorado speed climbing records.)

www.mountainzone.com

www.everest2000.com

www.rayjardine.com

www.supertopo.com

www.touchstoneclimbing.com

www.ccrank.com

www.rocklist.com

www.birthdaychallenge.com

www.inspirationforhire.com

HANS FLORINE

Hans Florine lives in California with wife Jacqueline, daughter Marianna, and son Pierce. Hans was a U.S. National Champion in Difficulty and Speed Climbing, a World Champion in Speed Climbing, and a three-time gold medalist in Speed Climbing at the X Games. He holds numerous speed records in outdoor climbing, from sport routes to alpine ascents. Hans competes in just about anything and was an All-American in the pole vault. He received a B.S. in Economics from California Polytechnic State University. For four years Hans was the executive director of the American Sport Climbers Federation, the governing body for competitive climbing in the United States. He describes himself as an Objectivist in the tradition of the writer Ayn Rand. He is an inspirational speaker, professional climber, writer, photographer, teacher, and guide.

BILL WRIGHT

Bill Wright is a software engineer who lives in Superior, Colorado, with his wife Sheri and two sons, Daniel Layton and Derek Logan. Bill spent nine years working in the Bay Area and climbing most of the structures in Yosemite. In order to balance his passions for climbing and family life, Bill has turned more and more toward speed climbing. Bill has climbed on three different continents and enjoys alpine climbing, big walls, scrambling, and cragging.